The
Black
Middle
Class

Sidney Kronus
University of Illinois

Charles E. Merrill Publishing Company
A Bell & Howell Company
Columbus, Ohio

Merrill Sociology Series

Under the editorship of
Richard L. Simpson
*University of North Carolina,
at Chapel Hill*

ISBN: 0-675-09218-3

Library of Congress Catalog Card Number: 79-148247

1 2 3 4 5 6 7 8 9 — 77 76 75 74 73 72 71

Printed in the United States of America

To my parents, Anne and Sidney, whose wisdom and tolerance shall
never be forgotten.

Acknowledgments

This study could not have been written without the help of many people, and it is with great pleasure that I acknowledge my indebtedness to them.

With my wife, Carol Lefson Kronus, I have shared a working partnership as a husband and a colleague for many years. Much of this book is an indirect result of her compassionate encouragement and intellectual stimulation.

The prime mover behind this study was Professor David Street and my gratitude to him can never be expressed adequately. I must simply say that without the benefit of his teaching, guidance, friendly advice and astute criticism, this book could not have been written.

Professors Morris Janowitz and Richard L. Simpson read earlier versions of this book and provided me with many valuable comments. Madeline Gates aided me greatly in editing and revising an earlier version of this study.

Special thanks are due to Edith Burkhalter and Maxine Rias for interviewing and to Patricia Gillen, Vivian Alsip, and Patricia Reedy for typing the manuscript.

Finally, it is a pleasure to state my indebtedness to the members of the black middle class who were willing to share their time and experiences with me so that I might better understand them. I am especially grateful to Robert Black.

Contents

Tables

1

Introduction

Well over a half a century ago, the great black historian, W. E. B. DuBois, wrote an important essay entitled "The Talented Tenth" (DuBois 1903, pp. 33-75). In this essay, DuBois argued quite eloquently that the future of the black race in America depended upon the ability and determination of its educated members to lead the masses of their people through the path of education to a position of productivity and respect in our society. He felt that higher education for the black man would produce a Talented Tenth—men and women of intelligence, sympathy, and knowledge, who would set the ideals of their community, direct its thoughts, and provide moral inspiration and character. He did not see education as simply providing skills for work as Booker T. Washington did, for he did not see the Talented Tenth as artisans, nor did he feel that education should be directed at moneymaking activities, for he did not feel that the Talented Tenth should lead by virtue of its pocketbook. He envisioned a segment of the black community that could teach life to his people — a Talented Tenth who would work as missionaries of culture and thought to uplift the spirit of an oppressed people. In short, he was describing a socially responsible and everexpanding black middle class.

This concern with the development of a black middle class is the inevitable consequence of the black man's sharing in the dominant values of white America's social class structure; and, it is a concern that should be of prime importance to those who are interested in the future of the black race in America. For the black middle class, with

1

its training, skills, and experience in coping with the white man's urban industrial society, must be seen as the primary motive force to integrate the millions of blacks who live within our borders. Many years ago, following the lead of DuBois, John Dollard emphasized the unique possibilities afforded the student of race relations by investigating the black middle class.

> There is a particular advantage in studying middle-class Negroes first in getting a view of the Negro caste. From them one can see both ways, back to the lower-class positions they have come from and forward to the full human status they aspire to but cannot reach. (1957, p. 449)

But what is the black middle class? Where did it come from? How does it fit into the current American social and economic structure? In order to answer these questions, we must look briefly into the development of black class structure in the United States.

The Foundation of the Black Middle Class

The black class structure in American society had its roots in the plantation system of the rural South. More particularly, it began within hated confines of that peculiar institution — slavery. The practitioners of slavery in America made it a point to completely destroy any fabric of African social structure and heritage. All classes were leveled and all tribes became merged into one common category: the slave, and soon the distinction between the term "slave" and "Negro" disappeared and one became synonomous with the other. Older men and women may have cherished and re-created in their minds memories of their African homeland but the world around them forced them to speak a new language, work in a prescribed manner, and adapt to the ways of life of the white man. The second generation, the children of the forced migrants, soon lost track of the bits and pieces of African lore and history that their parents tried to pass on, and very quickly a whole series of cultures and civilizations were lost. In their place remained a commodity, a laboring human to be bought and sold as economic necessity demanded.

It follows then that the class structure that emerged for the black man emerged from the economic necessities of plantation life. Three more or less distinct categories of labor for black people were generated by the plantation which gave rise to their social structure. These categories were (1) field hands (by far the largest group), (2) artisans and craftsmen, and (3) household servants.

Lowest on the social ladder were the field hands—those unfortunates who were required to work the land from sun up to sun down usually under the watchful eye of the oft-times sadistic overseer or field boss. This segment of black "society" had the least opportunity to come in contact with the socializing influences of the white community. Their contact with whites was pretty much relegated to brief and demeaning encounters with the overseer, a figure described by slave owners as "poor white trash."

More well-off, in terms of working conditions, than the field hands, but not so well-off as the house servants, were the artisans and craftsmen. These included the blacksmiths, carpenters, masons, and other skilled and semi-skilled workers who built and maintained the capital equipment of the plantation. This group worked with greater autonomy than the field slaves, often without an overseer, and in many instances were hired out to work in the villages and cities during a slow period on the plantation. The nature of their work and its proximity to the mansion as well as occasional monthly sojourns in the towns gave them more than a glimpse of the white man's world.

At the top of the black social ladder on the plantation were the household servants. This group of men and women, butlers and valets, cooks and maids, were in constant contact with their white masters. They were in the best position to see in intimate detail how the upper class white man thought, worked, and played. There was one other "class" in the black society of the South and these were the "free Negroes"—men and women who had purchased their freedom by diligent effort or who had been set free by some liberal planter, because of some heroic deed, or more frequently because of long years of faithfulness.

As a consequence of the sexual exploitation of black women by white men, mulattoes appeared very quickly in the slave-holding areas of the United States. These mulattoes, especially the lightest colored and those with the most Caucasian physical characteristics, were treated far better than fresh arrivals from the African continent. The highest proportion of house servants were mulattoes. So, very early in the development of black social structure, the quality of "lightness" became associated with the highest social and occupational class. Light-skinned mistresses of slave owners and their children were granted petty privileges in the great household and the lightest skinned were given their freedom more frequently than their darker brethren.

Soon, mulattoes began to see themselves as a distinct high-status group within the black community. After the Civil War and the end of slavery, the former household slaves continued to work in the occupations for which they were trained. The combination of lightness of skin and of working in close proximity to whites was the major determinant of social standing in the free black communities.

The black middle class, then, was born on the plantations of the Old South and was comprised of light-skinned black people who worked almost exclusively with whites. They took on the values and life styles of their former white masters as much as they could. They strove to obtain education, placed high emphasis on correct manners of speech and dress, and tried very hard to disassociate themselves from the mass of illiterate, unskilled blacks. The nascent black middle class, like any middle class, preoccupied itself with securing its position.

From the beginning of this century until the early 1940s blacks developed a sort of parallel social structure in our society. Due to segregation policies, the educated members of the black middle class— the doctors, lawyers, and businessmen, and in far greater numbers the teachers and ministers—lived and worked in an all-black environment. Others, such as the postal workers, trainmen, and servants, worked with whites. They consciously identified themselves as middle-class citizens and worked to provide themselves with a life style which included a home, a car, an education for their children and, if they were highly successful, an elaborate vacation or a summer place.

In summary then, the black middle class was born in the rural South. Its identifying characteristics were light skin and either work that put its members in contact with whites or professional and business-trained people who provided services within the black community. The identifying characteristics of the black middle class have historically been centered around color and occupation. Leaving aside for a moment the factor of color, which is highly related to social status, we will look at a brief overview of the socioeconomic position of blacks in our society relative to whites.

Socioeconomic Status[1]

Although black people have traditionally used different criteria from whites for evaluating one another, the trend today is toward an increasing acceptance of the three main criteria of social status that are used

in the general community. Thus education is more frequently emphasized than any other status element, followed by occupation and income,
respectively. Other criteria which were mentioned in the past but
which are in a state of flux today, are (in order of importance):
respectability or morality, refinement or "culture," skin color or white
ancestry, family background, and property ownership (Glenn 1963,
p. 647). The three most important factors determining the socioeconomic status of blacks will be examined to determine the position
of black persons in our society relative to whites.

In a highly industrialized nation, such as the United States, education is the key factor in obtaining a job, and it is increasingly becoming
the measure of the man. Education to a large extent determines what
a man can do and is the best single indicator of what a man will do. As
early as the turn of the century, W. E. B. DuBois recognized the importance of educated individuals for a group of people when he asked:

> How then shall the leaders of a struggling people be trained and
> the hands of the risen few strengthened? There can be but one
> answer: The best and most capable of their youth must be schooled
> in the colleges and universities of the land. (1903, p. 45)

He felt that the college-bred black man "is as he ought to be, the group
leader, the man who sets the ideals of the community where he lives,
directs its thoughts and heads its social movements" (DuBois 1903, p.
54).

For blacks, obtaining a good education remains difficult, but the
number of well-educated black persons has increased markedly in
recent decades. Following the Civil War, 80 percent of the blacks in

---

[1]For a detailed picture of the socioeconomic position of the Negro middle
class in the United States, see the following references: U.S. Department of Com-
merce, Bureau of the Census, *Current Population Reports*, Series P-20, No. 194,
February 19, 1970, p. 1; U.S. Department of Labor, Bureau of Labor Statistics,
U.S. Department of Commerce, Bureau of the Census, and U.S. Department of
Health, Education, and Welfare, Office of Education, in *The Social and Economic
Status of Negroes in the United States, 1969,* BLS Report No. 375, Current Popu-
lation Reports, Series P-23, No. 29, p. 53; Department of Health, Education, and
Welfare, Office of Education, *Equality of Educational Opportunity, 1966* in
Statistical Abstract of the United States 1969, National Data Book and Guide to
Sources, 90th edition, p. 125; U.S. Department of Labor, Bureau of Labor Statis-
tics in *Employment and Earnings,* Bureau of Labor Statistics, vol. 16, No. 11,
May, 1970, p. 37; and U.S. Department of Commerce, Bureau of the Census,
Current Population Reports, Series p-60, No. 66, December 23, 1969, p. 32.

the United States were totally illiterate and living primarily in the rural South, many possessing no land. The majority of the black families today have risen above this level. Black Americans are now more urbanized than the white population and less than a tenth of the black labor force remains in agriculture.

The greatest increase in the educational level of black people has occurred in the last few decades. At the time of the Second World War, the average black person had completed less than six years of formal education (Killingsworth 1969, p. 206) but by 1969 the median number of school years completed by blacks twenty-five years old and over had risen to slightly over nine and one-half years, and more than one in twenty had completed college. While in 1964 only 234,000 blacks were enrolled in college throughout the country, by 1968 the number had nearly doubled with 434,000 blacks attending institutions of higher learning. Most blacks go to predominantly black colleges which are in many ways inferior to the predominantly white colleges and universities (Broom and Glenn 1965, p. 93; U.S. Department of Commerce, Business and Defense Services Administration 1966, pp. 45-50), yet the massive efforts by both public and private universities to recruit black students in the 1970s should change in an upward direction both the number of black persons going to college and the quality of college training they receive. In fact, in 1965 nearly 51 percent of the black students attending college were enrolled in institutions outside the South.

With a rise in the educational attainment of blacks, it is not surprising that they have also risen in the occupational structure of society. By almost any measurement used, the movement of a worker from agriculture into some non-agricultural employment is a rise in the occupational structure. In 1890, nearly 90 percent of black workers were concentrated in agriculture and domestic service occupations.

> The greatest change in the occupational status of Black people occurred between 1940 and 1960, when federal, state and municipal governments enacted laws forbidding the traditional discriminatory employment practices against Negroes. As a result of increasing employment opportunities, significantly greater numbers of Blacks were employed in white-collar and skilled occupations. (Pinkney 1969, p. 77)

The growth in the percentage of blacks in white-collar occupations during the period from 1940 to 1970 has been significant. Over one-fourth of the gainfully employed blacks in the United States are working in white-collar occupations, designating them as middle class, although most notable is the rise in clerical and sales occupations, the least prestigeful and lucrative of the white-collar occupations. The growth in the professional and technical categories is due for the most part to the greatly increased number of black teachers and social workers (Hare 1962, pp. 104-25).

The federal government has been at least in part responsible for the occupational rise of the black people in a very direct manner: they disproportionately employ them. And although most are at the lower end of the pay scale, the opportunity is given to blacks for white-collar employment. For example, in 1964 blacks comprised less than 11 percent of the total population in the United States and 10 percent of the labor force, but they accounted for 13.2 percent of all federal workers. Within the federal government, blacks tend to be connected with such agencies as the Government Printing Office, the Federal Services Administration, the Veterans Administration, the Department of Labor, and the Department of Health, Education, and Welfare. Each of these agencies maintains a 20 to 40 percent black labor force.

The black businessman has felt the repercussions of the changing pattern of race relations and he has found that catering to the segregated black market has become less profitable as the acceptance of segregation has declined in recent years. For example, between 1950 and 1960 the total number of black businessmen declined from about 43,500 to 32,400, a decrease of nearly one-fourth. The number of black-owned restaurants declined by one-third and a similar pattern can be seen for black funeral directors and barbers. This gradual decrease in the number of black small business enterprises is a consequence of the general economic trend in the United States as well as a reaction of decreased segregation, for corporations show much greater rates of return in comparison with small independent business organizations (Pinkney 1969, p. 80). But black businessmen are carving out and expanding areas where they have an advantage. During the sixties the black community felt that the general press was not responsive to their needs and by 1965 there were over 150 newspapers and magazines published by black-owned companies (Pinkney 1969, p. 85). Other efforts directed at building black capitalism during the late sixties and early seventies may produce an upswing in black business, but it is too early to tell.

From this discussion it may be concluded that the overall position of blacks in the occupational structure has improved very substantially since 1940, which would seem to indicate a similar increase in black income, the third major criterion for social evaluation and determination of class. In 1939 black families had a median annual income from wages and salaries of $489. This was 37 percent of the white median. By 1968 in the United States black median family income was $5,360, approximately two-thirds that of whites. From this it is evident that both in absolute terms and in comparison with the white majority, black income has improved tremendously in the past quarter century.

Leonard Broom and Norval D. Glenn make the statement that "not only are Negroes concentrated in the lower-paying occupations; they generally earn less than whites in the same occupations" (1965, p. 113). While this may be true, if we select $7,000 per year or more as a "middle class" family income, then approximately 37 percent of all black families in this country can be classified as middle class, with nearly one in five earning more than $10,000.

From the preceeding discussion of the education, occupation, and income of black Americans, it is evident that at the end of the 1960s and early 1970s the United States has witnessed the emergence of a significant black middle class. Excluding the South, approximately 20 percent of all black people graduate from high school or beyond, one-quarter work in white-collar occupations, and about 20 percent earn more than $10,000 a year, and these figures are rising. So, one can say with certainty that not all black Americans are poverty cases.

But social class as a concept implies more than just a black person's relationship to the economic structure of society as measured by educacation, occupation, and income. It includes, to a greater or lesser degree than in the white community, style of life and family background. This is due to the fact that the blacks are overrepresented in the lower class, and high income and occupational status are more than in the white community. Therefore, social stratification tends to be heavily based on behavioral patterns and social factors (Pinkney 1969, p. 68). The middle status black person, according to white standards, ranks above most other blacks, enjoying high prestige in the black community. However, when he judges his status in relation to whites, he finds himself somewhat lower in rank.

So, then, the black middle class is distinct within the black community due to its economic and social position which sets it above the mass of the black population. But what of their life styles, their goals and aspirations in life? What are their values? How do they live?

Life Style of the Black Middle Class

As opposed to the plethora of statistics on the demographic and socio-economic position of blacks in the United States, there is relatively little information concerning the life style of the middle-class black. The accounts that do exist can be divided into two groups. The first group is the "Classics": John Dollard's *Caste and Class in a Southern Town,* Gunnar Myrdal's *An American Dilemma,* St. Clair Drake and Horace Cayton's *Black Metropolis,* and E. Franklin Frazier's *The Negro Family in the United States* and *Black Bourgeoisie.* These works describe the life style of the black middle class as it existed during the first half of the twentieth century, before the major gains in civil rights and before the middle class had increased in size. Although these accounts vary due to differences in decades and differences in location of the group under study, southern as opposed to northern locations, certain themes persist throughout these five books.

The first of these themes revolves around middle-class values and standards of conduct. Education has been described as almost "an obsession" for middle-class blacks. Going on to college or some sort of post high school training was a very high priority goal since the completion of higher education maximizes the possibility of economic success and stability. Strict sexual codes were maintained with a strong emphasis placed on giving respect to females. The value placed on moral obligations and a respectable way of life led to a low rate of promiscuity with legal marriage and marital fidelity as the usual state of affairs. Marriage was not taken lightly. Middle-class blacks were very careful to see that their children engaged in social activities with only those suitable for marriage, namely, other middle-class children or responsible working-class children of good moral background and character. Often, children were somewhat spoiled as parents over-extended themselves to make certain their children went to the right parties, the right schools, and that they had enough money and a fine wardrobe to insure their acceptance in the group. Even though family size was limited so that children could be well taken care of, the economic burden of children motivated many of the wives of middle-class blacks to work in order to provide additional income. This was much more common in the North than the South for, in the South, leisure on the part of the woman was a sign of superior social status. Also, home ownership and the ownership of other tangible property such as automobiles, large radios, and telephones was greatly valued by this group since these too were symbols of higher social status that set the middle class apart from the rest of the black community.

Finally, most members of the middle class were "church going" people. They tended to organize and support their own churches, often of the same denomination as the masses but quite different in discipline and program of functions. Middle-class churches were much more sedate than those of the lower class. There was little emotionalism, even to the point of refraining from singing spirituals. The musical emphasis was placed on "taste" and "the best" so that soloists, both voice and piano, were much more common than congregational singing of spirituals.

Basically, this theme held that personal standards of conduct and behavior of the black middle class were modeled after the prevailing norms of the middle-class white community which stressed responsibility, the striving for and leading of the "respectable" life.

Color and shades of pigmentation which strongly influence the nature of social relations provide the basis for the second theme: pigmentocracy. The earliest studies of skin color among blacks (see Reuter 1918; Woodson 1934; Caliver 1933) show very clearly that from the earliest times, lightness or the admixture of white blood was the hallmark of higher-status blacks. It was the sign of the old established mulatto families which, relative to the bulk of the black community, indicated persons of better education, higher income, stable family traditions, and in general respectability and culture. Therefore, fair skin became a symbol of high status and as such was highly valued by those black persons who either desired to maintain or achieve a high status position.

As a consequence of this high value placed upon light skin, marriage patterns generally followed along the lines of lightness. Men and women attempted to find partners of the same or lighter shade, thereby retaining or improving their status. Through this means, darker members of lower strata who had achieved better educations and higher occupational status could ascend to the middle class and solidify their position by marrying a lighter spouse. Reflective of this process is the finding of practically all of the studies of skin color and marriage among the middle class that, in a large proportion of the families, the man is darker than the woman — the natural result of American courtship patterns, black or white, where the decision to determine one's spouse resides overwhelmingly with the male. The course of these events led Frazier to conclude: "Thus color loses its caste basis as represented by older mulatto families, and a brown middle class seems to be emerging" (1967, p. 321).

The third theme deals with the social psychology of the black middle class, a social psychology in which the main components are: (a) their attempt at maintaining a white middle-class standard of behavior, (b) lack of recognition and acceptance by whites, and (c) the value placed on "whiteness" which as a corollary places a negative value on anything specifically identified with being black, be it physical or cultural.

The social psychology of the middle-class black revolves around an identity crisis. Clear expression of this is found in E. Franklin Frazier's basic argument that the black bourgeoisie have broken with their folk tradition and rejected the black masses in their quest to gain "white" status. But whites have rejected them, leaving them with feelings of inferiority, insecurity, guilt, frustration, and ambivalence about black and white (Frazier 1962, pp. 24-25, 213). In the absence, then, of meaningful, mutually rewarding social contacts with whites or lower-class blacks, they have developed a life style of social contacts and social events devoted to trivialities. Parties, with the "right" people (whites or other middle-class blacks), elaborate cotillions and costume balls analogous to the Southern upper-class white variety, poker parties and other varieties of gambling, and "high fashion" events took on an aura of obsession for the black bourgeoisie. Personality and individualism dominated over any sense of collective responsibility and action to "help the race."

The social psychology of their world of work was strongly influenced by their relations with whites. Rejected by white people in the middle class, the middle-class black experienced powerful feelings of inferiority and insecurity. Many were educated in all-black schools where the standards of excellence were lower than in white schools. Others attended integrated schools where they were constantly reminded of their "place" and second-class citizenship. There developed from these rejections the notion that blacks could not compete effectively with whites in the work situation. As a result, they feared occupational competition and fashioned a defense mechanism which was "playing at work" (Frazier 1962, p. 213), not taking work seriously. This strategy, of course, only served to further reinforce the feelings of inferiority held by the middle-class black man.

The black middle class of the first half of the twentieth century then, by virtue of their unique position in American society, could be identified by certain characteristics. As a group, they exhibited a strong faith in education and personal accomplishment. They were highly individualistic and placed heavy emphasis on personality. Within the black community they were quite isolated, due to their heavy orientation to their own class and their parochial middle-class society. Their values, culture, and almost total way of life was the best copy they could make from the white designs they so dearly cherished. There was no room in their lives for race as such. They pretended that it did not exist in the same way that they acted as though the black masses in the country did not exist. Their identity was based on a weak fabrication of denial of their past and an unsuccessful attempt to emulate the life style of upper-class whites. The summary of the classic accounts of this group reads as a pointed condemnation. With the exception of a handful of effective leaders, the educated white-collar black American was described as accommodating, unassertive, focusing on personality rather than achievement (Myrdal 1964, pp. 725-35, 786-88), frivolous, consumption-oriented, concerned with putting up a "front" (Drake and Cayton 1962, pp. 658-715), and finally, by its most severe critic, as ambivalent, immature, childish, frustrated, phony, false, self-hating, and suffering from "nothingness". because when Negroes attain middle-class status, their lives lose both content and significance (Frazier 1962, passim).

The black middle class changed significantly around the middle of the twentieth century. As we have shown earlier in this chapter, its size has increased due to the greater educational and occupational attainment of blacks. There had been a regional shift in the concentration of black people from the towns and rural areas of the South to the urban North during and after World War II. Beginning in 1941 with Franklin D. Roosevelt's executive order banning discrimination in government employment, through the monumentous decision of the Supreme Court in *Brown* vs. *Board of Education of Topeka* which declared segregation in public schools illegal, and culminating in the Civil Rights Acts of 1957, 1960, and 1964, the black man has won the battle for legal equality and has at the present time a virtual government on race relations (Franklin 1965, pp. 899-920).

These changes, both socioeconomic and legal, have affected the black middle class to such an extent that the descriptions of this group by earlier writers must now be questioned. The basis for this questioning is both theoretical and empirical.

First, it is obvious that given the broad range of occupation, education and income of this group, structural differentiation exists. This structural differentiation along with changes in the political and legal environment of the black man should theoretically bring about further changes in his social patterns and personality development. Myrdal postulates in his principle of cumulation that "on the whole, a rise in any single one of the Negro variables will tend to raise all the other Negro variables" (Myrdal 1964, p. 1066). This model of dynamic social causation can be observed from a psychological point of view. In accord with Hartmann's theory that reality and environment shape the ego and underlying drives (Hartmann 1950, pp. 74-96; 1952, pp. 9-30), there should be lesser feelings of self-hatred and anti-white prejudice on the part of the blacks as well as increased group indentification, personal pride, and individual responsibility. In a broad sense, the environmental changes, coupled with the increase in the proportion of middle-class blacks, allow for greater differentiation than was evident in the past (Eisenstadt 1964, p. 375-85).

Gordon W. Allport in his model of minority group reactions to victimization also points to the possibility of increased within-group differentiation among the black middle class as well as perhaps a basic shift in the norm of reaction. According to Allport's model, minority group members may display visible ego defenses ranging from the basically intropunitive, evidencing symbolic status striving (playing at work and working at play) which conforms to the stereotype given in earlier studies, to the extropunitive, evidencing enchanced status striving (working at work and competing with whites) which, as we shall see in the next section, is much more prevalent in the black middle class of today (Allport 1958, pp. 138-57). Allport and others contend that there may be a blending or mixing of response patterns because of the ambivalence and ambiguity of holding marginal status in the dominant society (Allport 1958, p. 156; Horney 1945, passim; Pettigrew 1964, pp. 27-54).

Thus, from a theoretical viewpoint, we should expect changes in the life style of the black middle class. This expectation is partially fulfilled by the precious few accounts that portray the black middle class' entry into the second half of the twentieth century.

Recent Analyses of the Black Middle Class

Only two books have focused on the black middle class since the writing of E. Franklin Frazier. The first of these is the *Black Anglo-Saxons* by Nathan Hare (1965). Hare, a disciple of Frazier, attempted to categorize individuals of the black middle class into twelve types on the basis of their attitudes and behaviors. However, none of his categories are mutually exclusive; at best they are quite arbitrary. Consistent with the *Black Bourgeoisie,* the overriding concern of *Black Anglo-Saxons* is with the "aping of the white man." In Hare's own words:

> This book is an exposé — a double exposure, if you will — of Black Anglo-Saxons on one hand, on the other, the white norms they so blindly and eagerly ape . . . I have used these categories as chapter division, although, perforce, they are somewhat arbitrary and overlap one another. Probably all Negroes, the author included, at some time or another have been guilty of Black Anglo-Saxon behavior in some sphere; others belong in several categories simultaneously or in sequence. Few are all types all of the time. (1965, p. 16)

Much like the work of Frazier, Hare's monograph gives one insight into the problems of the black middle class living in a white society. The conclusions are based, however, on personal anecdotes, hearsay, and unsystematic content analysis of mass media. From this exposé, one can only conclude that the black middle class of today is not significantly different from the black bourgeoisie described by Frazier. In contrast to Hare's monograph, Eli Ginzberg's book *The Middle Class Negro in a White Man's World* (1967) and practically every other piece of social science research on the black middle class reveals very important changes in their life style and world view. These changes center around a positive self-identity for the middle-class black person, an identity that has been variously labeled as the "New Negro" and the "New Negro Creed."

The first of these is the interracial stance which is changing from the traditional pattern of attempting to emulate "whiteness" by courting whites, using white role models, accepting white domination, and degrading the black man and his uniqueness to a position that now values the inherent human dignity of the black man, his culture, and the capabilities that he has as a man.

The second change is in the intraracial stance and is the shift from the class orientation of the past (the middle-class black for the black middle class) to a mass orientation (the middle-class black for the black man) which results in a psychological shift from that of self-hatred to pride in oneself.

It is no longer fashionable for the black man to accommodate himself to the desires of the white man. "Uncle Tomism" in all forms of attitude and behavior is no longer acceptable to the majority of middle-class blacks (Wilson 1960, pp. 66-67; Williams 1964, p. 253; Watts 1964, pp. 110-11; Hughes and Watts 1964, pp. 112-15). They are demanding the right of personal self-determination in politics, education, housing, and occupation. They are unafraid to compete with whites on an equal, serious basis (Back and Simpson 1964, pp. 68-68; Ginzberg 1967).

The middle-class black is taking an ever-increasing role in the championing of the black man's rights in America. High participation in the civil rights movement (Brink and Harris 1964, pp. 203-4) as well as strongly militant yet pro-integrationist tendencies (Marx 1967, pp. 124-26) are established patterns among middle-class black people today. They are less likely to disparage their race and especially the lower class than they have been in the past (Noel 1964, p. 81). According to Thompson's study of the black leaders in New Orleans (1963), there was a marked shift in the efforts of this group from the class orientation of the past where they concerned themselves with trying to raise the cultural level of blacks to a mass orientation where the issues centered around welfare issues and police brutality — clearly the major concerns of the black lower class.

However, a word of caution must be interjected here lest we become too easily swayed by the weight of these recent accounts of the "New" black middle class. We must ask ourselves, how meaningful are these changes in inter- and intraracial disposition? Aren't there, indeed, powerful holdovers from the past? Who really benefits most from this seemingly new posture of the black middle class? The ambivalence and complexities of any minority group or segment of a minority group rarely allow clear interpretation. Harold Cruse, in his treatise on the black intellectual, re-introduces the classic Frazierian theme of the personal self-interest of the middle-class black man when he states, "No matter how you view it, the integration movement is run by the middle class who, even when they are militant and sometimes radical, twist the meaning of integration to suit their own aspirations" (Cruse 1967, p. 312).

We can now ask ourselves *the* central question: *What is the black middle class really like in the third quarter of the twentieth century?* Secondarily we can ask, what do they think? How do they live? What are some of the differences between people in this group? Are they more like the black bourgeoisie or the New Negro? From this central question and its subsequent derivations we can arrive at three basic propositions to be examined in this book. In Chapter 2 we will test the proposition that the black middle class of the 1960s and 1970s does not conform well to the earlier depictions of them, especially to that of E. Franklin Frazier's *Black Bourgeoisie*. In Chapter 3 we will test the proposition that internal structural differentiation among the black middle class has advanced to the point where blue-collar blacks can no longer be included

in the operating definition of the black middle class. In Chapters 4 and
5 we will test the proposition that the black middle class can be differentiated into four analytic types along the two dimensions of interracial
and intraracial sentiments. Chapter 6 contains the life history of a middle-
class black man which in many respects portrays the dominant themes in
the life of a middle-class black American as well as the subtleties and
ambiguities that almost defy social science conceptualization. In the final
chapter we will attempt to integrate the materials brought to bear on
this subject.

The primary source of data for this study is a sample of sixty black
males employed in white-collar occupations and twenty black males
employed in blue-collar occupations. The respondents were chosen from
the Chatham community area of Chicago which is an all-black residential
area on the South Side.[2]

Because of the essentially social psychological element in this study
we decided to use a predominantly open-ended interview through which
we could capture in the respondent's own words his feelings on various
topics (see Appendix A for a copy of the schedule). We quote liberally
from these materials so that the reader may interpret directly from the
respondent's comments. Few persons who have engaged in the interview
process would disagree with the notion that the gaining of the respondent's confidence is absolutely necessary to obtain valid results. Given
the tense racial situation in this country and the greater ease with which
women can obtain sensitive information, three black females collected
all of the interview data with the exception of the elite perspectives presented in Chapter 7 which were obtained by the author after the data
analysis was completed.

_____

[2]It is true that since all of the respondents live in an all-black area it could be
argued that these are not the most integration-oriented persons in the black community. This could be a source of bias if it were not for the fact that at the time
two-thirds of them moved to this community, it was at least 50 percent white. This is
a problem faced by almost all blacks who live in large metropolitan areas. When
black people move in, whites move out, and residential integration is only a tempo-
rary phenomenon. At present, for example, the Crenshaw district near Watts in Los
Angeles is experiencing the same thing. Middle-class blacks are moving in at such a
rapid rate that soon this "integrated" area will become all black despite the efforts of
some of the white residents to prevent it. This situation is caused not only by the fear
that whites have of blacks in their neighborhoods, but also by the pressures of the
housing market. Middle-class blacks have so few opportunities to purchase good
housing that when an area is opened up to them, they quickly dominate it. Although
there are a few exceptions to this pattern, most notably the Hyde Park area of Chicago, racial succession and not integration is the dominant theme of urban ecology
in America today.

In the 1960s and 1970s vast amounts of economic and human resources have been expended to study the black poor but relatively little research effort has been directed toward the middle class or the stable, non-poverty working class. We have some indications of the rapidly changing nature of the black middle class but we really do not know much about them as of 1970 and precious little as of the 1960s, and this knowledge is needed. Our sixty interviews and one life history may seem a weak foundation for an investigation of such a broad nature. Yet, our findings are meaningful in their own right since they are derived from such an important segment of the black community. Further, by tracing patterns through these materials and analyzing the complexities contained in them we should have a better grasp of the black man's difficult task of "making it" in the white man's world.

2

The Changing Picture
of the
Black Middle Class

Any scholarly research effort directed at the black middle class owes a tremendous intellectual debt to E. Franklin Frazier's ground-breaking monograph, *Black Bourgeoisie.* Frazier, through his scholarly research and personal experiences, provided the most comprehensive description of the black middle class that had ever been accumulated. It remains, even today, a base point of departure for the study of middle-class black Americans.

E. Franklin Frazier's classic description saw the black middle class as predominately composed of light-colored aristocrats, descendants of house slaves and of the landed *gens de couleur,* and a small proportion of darker, intergenerational-occupationally mobile persons without a claim to favorable ancestry. He defined this group very broadly in socio-economic terms; occupationally, it ranged from craftsmen and clerks to professionals, and it included those with incomes in excess of $2,500 as of 1949 and practically any black American who had a high school education or some sort of specialized training (Frazier 1962, pp. 45-76). This class of blacks is described as people who live in a world of make-believe and unreality, seeking recognition only from the white community. They avoid competition with whites for fear they will be treated objectively, a situation with which they are too insecure to cope. Therefore, they live beyond their means, emphasize social life and consumption, reject their race, and take no interest in leadership. In short, "their lives generally lose both content and significance" (Frazier 1962, p. 195).

This description is based upon data and personal knowledge which was accumulated before the birth of the civil rights movement in the late 1950s and prior to the major changes in the labor force composition of blacks. There are no adequate measures of the impact of the civil rights movement on the lives of the middle-class black man. We can say with some certainty, however, that the increase in the proportion of blacks holding white-collar positions indicates that there has been an influx of mobile persons into the middle class. Given the stable reproduction rate of the middle class, this increase necessarily has had to come from occupational mobility.

This occupational mobility, or in broader terms social mobility, has important consequences for individual and group action. Durkheim (1897), in his classic study of suicide, saw social mobility as having disruptive effects for the individual and society. He felt that the social bonds of people were weakened by mobility and concomitantly, the basic institutions of society were weakened as well. This led him to look for and find greater rates of suicide among groups with higher rates of social mobility. Here, however, we are dealing with individuals who have made socioeconomic achievements within the social system and have not suffered losses. Their personal and social well-being is greater than that of their families. Therefore we could expect, contrary to Durkheim, that instead of contributing to social instability, upward social mobility by widening individual and group horizons can make a positive contribution to social stability. Indeed, Parker and Kleiner (1966, pp. 267-96) in a broad study of mental health in the black community of Philadelphia found that persons who had experienced upward occupational and educational mobility manifested lower rates of mental disorders than did downwardly mobile or stable, non-mobile persons. Whether the influx of these "mobile" persons will have positive or negative effects on the overall composition of the black middle class is an empirical question. Yet we can expect some effect. This change in the social base of the black middle class as well as the growth in numbers should produce a larger and more differentiated group. These demographic changes coupled with the black man's role in the forefront of the "revolution of rising expectations" present a new and unique set of factors operating in the black community.

As a consequence of these changes, one would expect a different description of the black middle class to be meaningful. Frazier himself was cognizant of this, for he stated in 1962:

> The most recent accessions to the Negro middle class . . . do not have the same social background as the black bourgeoisie in my study who

represent a fusion of the peasant and the gentleman. Although they have been influenced by the genteel tradition, on the whole, their background is essentially that of Negro folk. Very seldom can they or their parents claim ancestors among the mixed-blooded aristocracy which was free before the Civil War. (1962, p. 12)

It is the purpose of this chapter to begin to present this new picture of the black middle class that Frazier identified but did not define. We will look at the social and social psychological characteristics of our sample as a whole to see how they measure up to the picture that E. Franklin Frazier so vividly describes in the *Black Bourgeoisie*. We will argue that our data on the contemporary black middle class do not fit the classic picture previously presented. Rather, these data fit much better into the model of a black middle class which represents responsible, striving, realistically-oriented people, working within the context of a larger white society and evidencing little of the unreality and falseness of life attributed to them.

Our major focus in this chapter will be on the middle-class blacks' attitudes and behavior in the areas of life style patterns, interracial and intraracial positions, and political stance. However, before presenting these materials, we will look first at the demographic, socioeconomic, and family structure characteristics of our group as a whole to provide a base line with which to determine whether life style patterns are realistic and responsible or irresponsible and phony.

Demographic and Socioeconomic Characteristics

It is indeed noteworthy that the middle class does not rest upon the "traditional" base. Two-thirds of the individuals interviewed were sons of fathers who worked in blue-collar manual occupations. Also significant is the fact that three-fourths of the sample were brown (48 percent) or dark brown (27 percent) in color as rated by black interviewers. These facts indicate that status has not often been gained by ascription to color; rather, achievement, motivation, and striving are likely to have been the primary factors in determining middle-class status.

In Chapter 1, we presented national statistics which document the rise in income and education for the national black population as well as provide figures for our sample which indicated that the income and educational levels of this group were quite high. A fairly high level of family income, for example $1,000 per month, which would be representative of our sample, may provide the wherewithal for a comfortable style of life depending upon the size and structure of the family.

Family Structure and Size

For blacks in the United States, stable family life has been problematic due to the precariousness of their legal, but especially their economic, position. The nature of slavery militated against the development of a stable family system. After slavery, the legal influences on family instability for black people declined but the economic disabilities remained, making it very difficult for black men to provide the basic necessities of life for their families. This led to widespread family disorganization and sexual promiscuity. Nevertheless, the more economically successful blacks — usually mulattoes with higher levels of education and skills — were able to maintain much more stability of family life by patterning their family relations after those of middle-and upper-class whites. Historically (see Frazier 1966), as well as today (see U.S. Bureau of Census 1966), blacks in the United States have had higher rates of broken families, female-headed households, and illegitimacy than whites but mainly among the lowest income families (Moynihan 1965). Middle-class blacks, in comparison, have avoided family disorganization by providing an adequate level of income, adhering rigidly to traditional sexual norms, and having small families.

The families in our sample illustrate this pattern of stability very well. Of the sixty male household heads, forty-seven are presently living with their original spouse, eight have been divorced but remarried, and the remaining five are living without a female being present. Of these last five, two are widowed, and three are separated from their wives. The rate of divorce here (eleven out of sixty) may seem high, yet all but three have remarried which indicates a strong adherence to the prevailing norm of the nuclear family composed of husband, wife, and children.

Consistent with Frazier's description of the middle-class black family and contrary to the high fertility patterns of the black lower class, the sample as a whole shows a very low fertility pattern. In fact, over half of the families are not replacing themselves. Further investigation of estimated completed family size (number of children living plus the number expected) shows that one-fourth of the families will have one child or none and 42 percent will have two, which leaves only about one-third who will have three or more children. This pattern of low fertility is indicative of families who see clearly the amount of personal and financial investment needed for children in an urban-industrial society. As one respondent remarked to the interviewer concerning completed family size,

CASE NO. 16   I expect to see my two children through college and to be honest, even with my income (over $12,000 per year) it's going to be a strain.

In sum then, we can say that as a whole the sample is well-educated, financially comfortable, and is composed of small families — a description which corresponds to Frazier's description of the black bourgeoisie. Yet there are differences. Our members are much more highly educated, they all hold white-collar occupations, and perhaps most significantly the majority of them are not light-skinned sons of middle-class families. Now to the heart of the matter: How do they live?

Life Style Patterns

The style of life of the middle-class black as depicted in previous studies ranges along a continuum from the stable, frugal, and hard-working family to the flashy, ostentatious type that lives way beyond their means and directs almost all of its efforts toward the search for excitement, glamour, and entertainment. Drake and Cayton's description of the middle class of Bronzeville (1962, pp. 658-715) is much closer to the former although they describe at great length the elaborate social life of Bronzeville's black middle class. Both Frazier (1962) and Hare (1965) lean much more heavily on the latter, describing an array of salacious, social climbing, and pleasure-oriented behavior engaged in by middle-class blacks. We turn now to some selected characteristics of life style to see which description is supported more by our data.

Home ownership has long been a traditional value in our culture and in and of itself cannot be considered an extravagance; rather, the size of the home is crucial. As previously mentioned, Chatham is composed of about one-third single-family dwelling units and two-thirds multiple-unit structures. Our sample shows just the opposite of this, with 31 percent living in apartments of seven rooms or less, and 68 percent living in a single-family house. This reversal of proportions in our sample is due to the white-collar requirement in our sampling, for the bulk of the apartment dwellers of Chatham do not fit our middle-class criteria. However, the size of these homes is quite modest. Of those respondents living in homes, not quite three-fourths live in structures of seven rooms or less, while slightly more than one-fourth live in homes of eight rooms or more.

The automobile plays an important role in our society with its emphasis on speed and mobility. It is looked upon by many as *the* status symbol and by some psychologists as man's alter ego. Blacks have been stereotyped as having a proclivity to purchase large flashy autos at the expense of the more basic necessities of life. This does not appear to be true in our sample. Eight percent do not own a car, and the majority, almost 60 percent, own only one. One-third of the individuals own two; however, if we recall that two-thirds of the families have two members in the labor force, it can be argued that two autos are more a necessity than a luxury, since two persons need transportation to work rather than one.

But what of the luxury, prestige automobiles? It is very difficult these days to determine just what a small car or a luxury car is. One can buy a Chevrolet for $2,500 or $5,000. If we consider the classic prestige autos, our sample reports ten: four Cadillacs and six Chryslers. These data are somewhat balanced by the report of seven Volkswagens and one Renault. Given the income levels of the people in our sample, we would argue that their expenditures for automobiles are far from frivolous.

Since Chicago has many miles of lake front, and boating is a popular sport, we are interested in seeing if the middle class spends much of its time and money on pleasure craft. Our respondents do not. Eighty-three percent do not even go to the lake, and of the ten individuals that do, only four own a pleasure craft.

For purposes of analysis we can group leisure time activities into two types. The first type, which Frazier calls "frivolous," includes drinking, playing cards and gambling, partying, and nightclubbing, with alcohol playing a major role (Frazier 1962, pp. 165-75). It was Frazier's contention that the majority of the black bourgeoisie participated in these activities to a very great degree or that these activities dominated the black bourgeoisie's leisure time pursuits.

It is our contention that these leisure time pursuits are no longer dominant in the black middle-class community; rather, other forms of activity predominate. These other forms are neither self-indulgent nor frivolous, but are better characterized as "family-centered, or self-improving." These activities include family activities, participation in cultural events, working around the house, and playing a musical instrument. For want of a better term we shall use the term "unwholesome" to characterize the first type in order to test the hypothesis that the leisure time pursuits of the black middle class more closely conform to the family-centered, self-improving variety than to the self-indulgent or frivolous.

A general over-view of the leisure time activities of the middle-class blacks in our sample indicates a propensity to participate in the "wholesome" group. Seventy-five percent make no mention of engaging in such activities as card playing, nightclubbing, or partying; in contrast, they participate once or more a week in family activities, sports events with friends or family, and singular activities such as reading, working about the house, or playing a musical instrument. Twenty percent of the individuals play an instrument. For those who did mention "unwholesome" activities, it appears that having parties once a week is the dominant activity, with three-fifths of the 25 percent who participate in activities classed as "unwholesome" reporting this. However, card playing and parties do not have to be considered unwholesome or frivolous in and of themselves; it is the excess of these activities that should be considered.

In summary, then, looking at unwholesome activities over the sample, we find that approximately one-quarter of the individuals evidence unwholesome social activity but that the majority spend their leisure time engaged in socially accepted activities with family and friends.

The final dimension to be investigated which affects the life style and consumption behavior of blacks is that of management of finances as measured by credit purchasing and saving. Credit buying is thought by many civil rights leaders to be the downfall of the black race. Uncritical acceptance of high interest rates and overextension of resources is considered to be a form of slavery differing in kind from physical bondage but similar in its debilitating effects (Davis, Gardner, and Gardner 1941, pp. 371-400). Table 2.1 presents the distribution of selected items purchased on credit.

A review of the literature of consumption patterns offers no standard with which to compare this distribution. We would argue, however, that the cost of purchasing a home and even an auto are high enough to justify time payment and generally prohibit a cash payment policy. Therefore, the high percentages of individuals who do use credit for these purposes are to be expected and justified. If we keep in mind the

TABLE 2.1
PERCENT DISTRIBUTION OF SELECTED ITEMS
PURCHASED ON CREDIT

Home[a]	98
Auto[2]	86
Television	33
Clothing	30
Food	2

[a]Percentage based only on those individuals who own the item.

income levels of these people, the purchase of an auto or a home on time is realistic and cannot be considered an overextension. Indeed, in this day and age of the charge-a-plate and the bank credit card, it is not surprising that approximately one-third of our sample purchases a television set and clothing on time.

In order to understand more clearly the individual's subjective feelings concerning the use of credit, we asked our group, "How do you feel about credit buying?" Eighty-eight percent of the respondents were for it and only 12 percent against. The most frequent response was that they were for it by necessity. Consider the following typical remark:

CASE NO. 47   I feel it is necessary. With the economic standards of today, people have to depend on credit. It is the lower income person's only means of survival, so I feel it is necessary. (a 41-year-old clerical worker who is purchasing his home, auto, and television set on credit)

Less typical is the individual who is strongly for credit buying:

CASE NO. 39   (Credit) is the life blood of the capitalistic system. If people stopped buying on credit the nation would crumble. (a 28-year-old drug salesman who is purchasing his home and auto on credit and is in the business of selling)

Finally, there is the individual who is strongly against it for reasons of loss of personal control and independence:

CASE NO. 21   I don't like it (credit). I don't like indebtedness. It takes away my independence. (a 45-year-old school teacher who is buying only his home on time)

If we compare now the picture of the style of life of our group with that of the black bourgeoisie of Frazier or the black Anglo-Saxons of Nathan Hare, it is apparent that the contrasts are more striking than the similarities. Our group seems to live in a much more modest and responsible manner than either the black bourgeoisie or the black Anglo-Saxons.

Interracial and Intraracial Positions

The reactions of a minority group, of which the black middle class is definitely a part, to their position in society can follow three fundamental forms: avoidance, aggression, and acceptance. These three guides for social interaction become highly complex when viewed from the perspective of how minority group members (middle-class blacks) react to the dominant group (whites) and from the perspective of how they react to members of their own group (blacks). Furthermore, if we consider that middle-class blacks may also react differently to members of different class levels within each racial group, the patterning of inter- and intraracial positions can become quite confused.

The major themes of reaction to whites by middle-class blacks follow the lines of acceptance and avoidance (Frazier 1962; Hare 1965; Drake and Cayton 1962). They have accepted the values of the larger society and try to pattern their lives so as to conform to these values. Most do not accept the position of inferiority that white society imposes upon them so they avoid contacts where this imposition may occur. And, being more affluent than lower-class blacks, they have more power and autonomy in isolating themselves. Frazier calls this the middle-class blacks' retreat into the world of "make-believe" (1962, p. 195), a world where they can produce an image of economic and cultural achievement far in excess of their actual situation.

The feelings of the middle class toward their own race traditionally have followed the forms of avoidance and aggression. Arnold Rose (1949, p. 89) has argued that by avoiding contact with blacks, especially lower-class blacks, the black man can escape the inferior identification of being black. This rejection of blacks by black men even pertains to the middle class. Very often middle-class blacks have denigrated the whole black race in the presence of whites with such statements as "we are a young race," casting themselves into the childlike image imposed upon them during the times of slavery. This pattern of self-reproach and self-hatred response can be seen as aggression displaced from the sources of frustration and insult, the white community, to one's own group. These feelings of self-hatred and inferiority are not effective nor rational responses. Rarely are they expressed unambiguously. However, they do reflect a tremendous source of strain in the black community which works against the formation of group solidarity, a strain which to some degree is also felt in the dominant white society. The attitudes of middle-class blacks toward the lower class and even themselves cannot be viewed totally within the framework of a racially mixed society. There are important class differences in values and life styles. Middle-class whites express many of the same feelings and actions of disassociation toward the white lower class.

These reactions of middle-class blacks, avoidance and acceptance of whites and avoidance and aggression toward their own race, have developed a situation where, until recent years, the black community has been relatively weak. For, any minority group which has internal differences, disorganized and ineffective institutions, and a poorly developed sense of sharing a common destiny will lack the sense of solidarity necessary to be effective in dealing with the dominant white society; they will more likely expend their energies in intragroup conflict which extracts few concessions or rewards from the larger social system.

However, in recent years there have been powerful changes in our society that bear directly upon the self-image of the black community. The educational and occupational status of blacks has improved. They have gained political offices and political power. The cooperative activity in the black community has increased and more and more one sees evidence of black group pride and a heightened sense of personal self-pride and self-determination. All of these factors indicate that the sense of identity for the black American is changing and that earlier formulations of his inter- and intraracial positions may no longer be appropriate. Let us look now at these positions taken by our sample.

Before looking into the attitudes and behavior that the middle class expresses toward whites, other middle-class blacks, and lower-class blacks, we must first establish a base line of existing interracial contact among our sample so that we can determine if proclivities for more contact have some real basis or are truly attempts to gain acceptance into the white community for social or frivolous reasons. Table 2.2 lists the frequency of contact with whites in everyday situations.

It is evident that interracial contact, or desegregation, has predominantly been achieved in the area of work and work only. Even

TABLE 2.2

PERCENT DISTRIBUTION OF FREQUENCY AND SETTING OF
CONTACT WITH WHITES

	Home	Work	Parties	Voluntary Organizations
None	38%	2%	17%	38%
Once a month or less	48	5	70	43
Once a week	8	7	12	13
Every day	5	87	2	2
No information	—	—	—	—
Total	100%	100%	100%	100%
N =	(60)	(60)	(60)	(60)

this is an overstatement if we consider that we are measuring only contact, however superficial. It may be that individuals interact quite intensely on the job, but contact can also exist of a few brief polite words exchanged in passing. Roughly, only about 15 percent of these middle-class blacks have any contact with whites in a meaningful way (once a week or more) outside the sphere of work. A note of caution should be included with this interpretation. These people are residents of Chatham which for all intents and purposes is an all-black residential area. It is reasonable to assume that those who have an intense desire for contact will not live in an all-black area but instead will pay the higher financial cost of living in an integrated area such as Hyde Park or Kenwood.

More significant than the fact that contact is at best minimal is the finding that over three-fourths of the sample said that the amount of contact was enough and in many cases too much. Consider the following responses, which range from definite anti-white feelings to a more moderate position based on a greater feeling of ease in the presence of blacks:

CASE NO. 45   It's quite enough for me, maybe too much. I think that the only problem is with the slowness and resistance to the civil rights movement. I feel fed up with whites in general. I feel a hostility toward them that I haven't felt before.

CASE NO. 53   Enough. I am unable to rid myself of prejudice for the white man because of what he has done to the Negro. Besides, I'm listening to Malcolm X.

CASE NO. 42   Through no fault of my own I am in close contact with them in my work and this is enough. We have nothing in common and I know they are nice and polite only because they have to be.

CASE NO. 30   Enough. Some of my experiences with whites have left a bad taste in my mouth, and the less contact with them, the better off I'll be.

CASE NO. 07   I'm not in love with white people and don't especially enjoy being around them. I just make a living that way.

CASE NO. 08   Enough. Every white person doesn't care to associate with Negroes, so I say everyone to his own taste. Those that I work with are regular and are as good friends as I would care to have.

CASE NO. 28   I like being around Negroes. It makes me feel at ease.

Only eight individuals desire more contact. Three desire it only in the area of work, and as one would expect, these persons are in the business of selling real estate and insurance and feel that greater contacts would increase their sales volume. The remaining five desire contact in social areas and give as their primary reason the need for increased interracial understanding. The following statement is exemplary of this position:

CASE NO. 44   I think there should be more in all areas because inasmuch as we are all here and have to live together, we should know more about each other than we know, and we should see more of each other and have more contact with each other in order that we may have a better understanding of each other as the races of man.

Since contact is such a general item, we also asked the respondents specific questions about the racial composition they would desire at work and where they lived, and why. The majority, two-thirds, felt that racial composition at work made no difference and their primary reason was that they would be willing to work with anyone as long as they were qualified. Only one in ten desired all or mostly all blacks in their work environment and gave as their reason that they felt more at ease working with blacks. The remaining quarter of the sample who desired a half-and-half or a mostly-white situation gave as their reasons: (1) they could learn from whites, (2) it would lead to greater racial understanding, and (3) it would create competition which would lead to more and better work. Therefore, in contrast to the notion that middle-class blacks are fearful of competing with whites, it appears that competition is not feared and in some cases is even encouraged and desired.

The preferences for residential racial composition show a slightly different pattern. It appears that more individuals desire an interracial residential neighborhood than an interracial work situation. There is a decided drop in the proportion who say that it makes no difference (from two-thirds for work to less than half for neighborhood) and an increase in the proportion who desire a half-and-half composition. One could interpret this as evidence that middle-class blacks do indeed want social interaction with whites and do seek the acceptance of the white community to the extent that two out of every five in the sample would want their neighborhood to be at least half white. However, the increased proportion desiring interracial composition of residence is completely explained not by the desire for social interaction with whites, but by the very realistic appraisal of the differential quality of community services between white and black areas. In the words of a 35-year-old college teacher, "I feel that police protection, schools, and services provided by the city are better in mostly white areas."

Since we have some evidence that courtship of the white community is not a prevailing norm, the question arises as to the bearing this has on the assertion that disparagement of their own race is a trait of the black middle class. To take a more psychological perspective, how prevalent is the concept of self-hatred within this group? Recent research conducted in this area (Noel 1964, p. 81) indicates that elements of group disparagement and self-hatred are present among the middle class but that it is not the dominant attitude. In an attempt to gain sensitivity in the measurement of group disparagement, two questions were asked about the respondent's feelings towards blacks in terms of two different classes; the middle class and the lower class (see Appendix A, Questions 23 and 24).

The respondents' opinions of their own class seem to bear out the group disparagement or self-hatred thesis propounded by Frazier. Thirty-six percent of the sample reported positive feelings toward their own class;

44 percent responded negatively; and 20 percent were ambiguous — that is, they spoke of both good and bad characteristics and would not take a clear position as to their judgments. Of those who held positive feelings toward the middle-class black, the intensity ranged from glowing images:

CASE NO. 16   I think the white-collar Negro is just as sharp and qualified as the middle-class, white-collar white man. But even at that, to be on the same level with the white man, he has to continue to be just a little bit better.

CASE NO. 03   Given half a chance they can become the best, as proven by the majority of cases.

CASE NO. 23   I feel that he is better educated, just as willing to work and make a showing in life as the white man in the same class.

to a positive but quite unemotional point of view:

CASE NO. 14   My opinion is that he is just a normal man that wants something out of life.

One-fifth of the sample gave both good and bad characteristics and were classed as ambiguous:

CASE NO. 41   I think he has earned his place in life (positive). But if they were to realize their position and help the lower class, we would progress much faster (negative).

The majority of the responses fell into the negative category. The following statements typify this majority position:

CASE NO. 28   Most of them seem kind of shoddy. They seem to shun the lower class.

CASE NO. 53   For the most part, he stinks. For the most part he is so interested in the material things of life for himself and his family that he has forgotten about the more unfortunate Negro. This is just the way it has to be because he is trapped in this vicious circle too.

CASE NO. 13   We have a tendency to be individualists. We should work together more and try to help our people to be creative.

CASE NO. 09   He is apathetic. He's too easily satisfied with his lot. By his limited association with white people he is afraid to push for greater gains for fear of losing what he thinks he has.

It is noteworthy that of those who do hold negative feelings toward the middle class, three-fourths do so not for reasons of incompetence, lack of education or qualifications, or personal consumption patterns. Nevertheless, the dominant theme is one of complacency, apathy, and inactivity in the area of helping the lower-class black — a frequent complaint of the leaders of the civil rights movement. However, the middle class is but one segment of the black population, and a small one at that. To be disparaging of the middle class is not to say that one is disparaging of the whole race. Let us look now at the feelings held toward the lower-class black man.

The majority of our sample reported that they did not hold negative feelings toward the lower class. Of the 63 percent who were not negative or ambiguous, only 10 percent gave truly positive statements:

CASE NO. 09   He is a fighter and not low by choice. He is the backbone and the future of the race of man because he will improve the lot of the poor blacks and white alike.

The remaining 53 percent were neither negative nor ambiguous about their feelings that the lower-class people are in the position they are in because they are victims of circumstances beyond their control. As one person put it:

CASE NO. 10   A victim of the white power structure. For the most part he is in an unfortunate social position in that he not only finds himself ostracized by the white majority but to some extent by the middle-class Negro.

Fifteen percent were ambiguous in their attitudes as seen by this typical statement:

CASE NO. 04   They are like lilies of the field. There is no guarantee that they can't rise up; some will, some won't.

About one-fifth of the sample responded in the negative vein with statements indicating the sentiment that the lower class does not do enough to help itself:

CASE NO. 26   That type of people are there because they don't want to do any better. You have that type in all races and it's just a part of modern civilization.

CASE NO. 46   They disgust me because sometimes I feel that these people don't want any better than they have. You could set them up on Lake Shore Drive and pretty soon they would have that torn down.

Having seen the amount of disparagement the middle class holds toward itself and toward the lower class, we can combine the two and arrive at a composite picture of race disparagement which will enable us to assess more effectively the prevalence of this feeling.

These data (Table 2.3) lend themselves to differing interpretations. To argue with Frazier and others, one could say that the fact that over 70 percent hold some feelings of race disparagement is evidence enough that the middle-class black does seek freedom by denying his identity and by disparaging the members of his own race (Hare 1965, p. 122). On the other hand, one could take the position that there is really a basis for criticism of both classes (middle and lower) and that the fact that over one-fourth of the sample does not criticize either class and almost two-thirds hold positive toward one of them is sufficient

TABLE 2.3
PERCENT DISTRIBUTION OF TOTAL RACE DISPARAGEMENT

Positive feelings toward both classes	27%
Positive feelings toward one class and negative feelings or ambivalence toward the other	63
Negative feelings toward both	7
Ambivalence toward both	3
Total	100%
N =	(60)

proof of the black man's willingness to identify himself as such and of his lack of disparagement of his race as a whole.

Dissatisfaction with the racial situation in the United States has been a dominant theme in black America for a long time. The black man who tried to change the pattern of black-white relations was considered "uppity" in the past; today he is considered militant. Black militancy is a fighting spirit or policy directed at changing the pattern of race relations that is very difficult to measure. Militancy may be violent or lead to violence, but necessarily so. The essence of black militancy is a willingness to pursue the goals of freedom and equality to the limits of one's moral constraints. If we proceed on the assumption that educated, middle-class blacks will not consider physical violence as a viable means to achieve these ends, then we can measure militancy by determining what steps short of violence a person will take or support to advance the cause of racial equality. We asked our sample whether they would agree or disagree with the statement, "In seeking to end racial discrimination, Negro Americans need to stop talking so much and to start more economic boycotts and other direct action." If we take a positive response to the statement as a militant viewpoint, then over half, 60 percent, of our sample are militant. About 20 percent would neither agree or disagree and the remainder disagreed. Therefore, we contend that if six out of every ten middle-class black people feel direct action is necessary, militancy is the dominant theme in the black middle class.

Further evidence that middle-class blacks do not deny their race but instead seek to advance it is their participation in the civil rights movement (Skolnick 1969, p. 130). Brink and Harris reported in 1963 (1964, p. 203) that almost 50 percent of the middle and upper income blacks in a national sample had actively participated in the civil rights movement. In our sample, only one-fourth of the individuals do not now contribute, nor have they ever contributed, in any way to the movement. Of the remainder, 43 percent have contributed their efforts in some way physically and 32 percent have contributed only money. In terms of effort, the most frequent mode of expression is marching and demonstrating, followed by organizing and doing fieldwork for a civil rights organization. Three respondents have served as officers, a chore involving a great deal more effort, and three persons have donated their profession musical talents to benefit performances in order to raise funds for their organizations.

These results seem highly inflated compared to the national scene on civil rights. It is possible that they are inflated because some of our respondents may have tried to present to the interviewer the image of "the civil rights participator" when in fact they had not participated at all. However, the fact that they are so predisposed lends validity to our assertion that the civil rights movement has had an impact on the black middle class and, where rejection of the race and especially the masses may have been fashionable in previous decades, it is definitely out of fashion now. But, as many of the black underclass of our country ask: Why don't they participate more? Why don't they give more of their time and energy to civil rights? Why do they seem so wrapped up in their own lives?

The answers to these questions about black middle-class involvement in civil rights can be found in the success syndrome of our society and in the relationship to the imperfect connection between legislative change and normative social change. Industrial society stresses personal accomplishment as the major route to achievement. Many middle-class blacks feel that additional legislation will have limited effectiveness in speeding up their future progress and opportunities. Many of the black leaders feel that this is why a significant proportion of the middle class have had only spectator roles in the civil rights struggle and why many active members are slowly disengaging themselves. An increasingly dominant view among middle-class blacks is that the most effective contribution that they can make in advancing the race is to assure their own personal success; to show the whites as well as the blacks that they are every bit as competent and motivated as their white counterparts. They see themselves in much the same perspective to the black lower class as the white middle class does in relation to poor whites. They deplore the conditions of the ghettoized black poor and will push forward in the most fruitful directions to alleviate their plight. Yet, with the exception of the small but ever-increasing segment that make their careers in community work, they see their goals best realized by improving their own circumstances. Black power is every bit as much gained by personal, economic, and political resources as it is by group organization.

Political Behavior

The final bit of evidence which supports the thesis that the black middle class is much more responsible and sophisticated in the conduct of their lives than other accounts have presented involves the area of political activity. It is well known that the Democratic machine controls the black vote in Chicago (Wilson 1960, pp. 49-52). Since the Republican party offers no viable alternative within this monolithic system, it is not surprising that only two individuals from our sample reported Republican affiliation. Significantly, over half of the remaining individuals would not align themselves with the Democratic party and instead classified themselves as Independents; one reported he was a Socialist. Their claim to participation in terms of voting in the 1964 election is almost total, with 95 percent reporting that they had voted in that election. But even more meaningful is the fact that only 23 percent voted for the straight Democratic ticket. Although over half voted mostly Democratic, they split their ticket indicating that they were voting more for single individuals than for the party.

James Q. Wilson (1960, p. 7) makes the statement that middle-class blacks have a distinct aversion to politics. Yet, our sample reports voting in substantial numbers, and over 20 percent have donated their time and energies in support of independent candidates to oppose William Dawson, the machine-controlled congressional representative for their district. It should be noted that 80 percent do not support Dawson, and one-half of these non-supporters are strongly against him. Consider the tone of the following opinions of Congressman Dawson:

CASE NO. 02   Stinks like Hell!

CASE NO. 07   He's a complete fake who has outlived his usefulness. None of the gains that the Negro in Chicago has made in recent years can be credited to Dawson. In all his years he has never been a public servant for his people.

CASE NO. 13   He has contributed nothing to his people. He is a fraud and an "Uncle Tom" for the white man.

CASE NO. 15   Mr. Dawson is not now nor has he ever been, a servant of the people. But he can't quit because he has done so much dirt and so little good.

CASE NO. 16   He is the biggest farce our people have for a leader. He is incompetent and corrupt.

CASE NO. 29   He is by far the worst charlatan. I cannot find the words to describe my contempt for the man. If he were in a war he would be a traitor. I doubt if he knows how to spell the word Negro.

Case No. 42   I think he should die and stop taking up good space. He has made enough money for himself and his flunkies.

It is also apparent that there is no great love held for the Daley machine itself, as three-fourths of the sample said they were against it. Their sentiments about it bear a striking resemblance to those felt about Dawson:

Case No. 15   I would rather say what I think of him to your husband. I don't think anything of him. Let's say he's a dictator.

Case No. 27   I would rather vote for Dick Gregory. They are perpetrators of fraud on the Negroes in this city. On the other hand, the Republicans didn't offer us anything better. (Note lack of alternatives).

Case No. 29   As long as the Daley machine is in power, there's going to be corrupt activity in everything. I think that the laws are enforced by the courts and as long as the Daley machine is in power, the courts are going to be corrupt so nothing is straight. The machine controls the powers that control everything in the city. So long as this is true, nothing is going to break it up.

Case No. 30   For the average Negro in the ghetto, it is worse under the Daley machine than it would have been under Jim Clark. The middle class doesn't exist for Daley because he has organized the ghetto Negro and coerced them.

The most lucid description of the politics of Chicago was given by a 29-year-old architect: "The Daley machine is a plantation-type political machine. I believe it's mostly corrupt and self-sustaining and Congressman Dawson is a number on the plantation."

Summary

To summarize briefly, we have argued that the black middle class is composed predominately of darker, occupationally mobile persons. In terms of life style and consumption patterns, they appear to live within their means, to take life seriously, and to accept their responsibilities to family, work, and community. As a whole, they have minimal desires for the superficial. Their position in the civil rights movement indicates a positive racial stance. Finally, their disassociation with the Democratic political machine of Chicago supports the idea that they are critical of the white power structure and seek a self-determined role in the advancement of their race.

This picture of the responsible middle-class black man is not new; rather, it is a validation of an idea propounded by more than one writer. As we mentioned earlier, Frazier himself forecast this finding in 1962 when he called attention to the recent infusion of "folk" elements into the black middle class (Frazier 1962, p. 12). Drake and Cayton foretold this configuration in their discussion of what they termed the "New Negro." They described the New Negro in terms of "racial advancement, stable family, disciplined public behavior, well educated, wanting to get ahead, and determined to be decent and skeptical of the intentions of most white people" (Drake and Cayton 1962, pp. 714-15). And in their assessment of Bronzeville in 1961, they spoke of the middle class as "demanding respectable public behavior, living in a conventional setting, and concerned with getting ahead" (Drake and Cayton 1962, p. XIX). Robin Williams, who investigated black communities in four larger white communities in each section of the nation, spoke of the emergence of the "New Negro Creed" centered in the younger, better educated members of the community (Williams 1964, p. 253).

The data we have presented support the notions of the New Negro and of the New Negro Creed. They also suggest that this element is not solely restricted to the younger segment of the black middle class. Since only 20 percent of our sample is composed of individuals under the age of thirty, and in many cases the number of individuals responding in New Negro terms exceeds 50 percent, it appears that this element rests on a broader base. In Chapters 4 and 5 we will investigate the differentiation along the inter- and intraracial dimension to see what factors other than age make up this base.

3

Comparisons
with
Blue-Collar Blacks

In this chapter we will compare the life styles of the blue-collar strata of the black population with that of the white-collar strata. Our definition of middle class, expressed in our sample selection, was based on the criterion of white-collar employment. Frazier's, as we mentioned earlier, was not. When he spoke of the black bourgeoisie's occupational basis, he discussed a range from physicians and lawyers, through officials and clerks, down to and including craftsmen and mail carriers (Frazier 1962, p. 47). In terms of income, Frazier used the 1949 figures of $2,000 and $4,000 per year (Frazier 1962, p. 49). In summary, Frazier's definition covered a very broad occupational base which included blue-collar and white-collar workers.

Drake and Cayton did not define middle-class status in socioeconomic terms; rather, they based their definition on life style and standard of living. In discussing the middle-class style of life, they stated:

> . . . neither occupation nor income is, in the final analysis, the decisive measuring rod. Rather, the middle class is marked off from the lower class by a pattern of behavior expressed in stable family and associational relationships, in great concern for "front" and "respectability" and in a drive for "getting ahead." All this finds an objective measure in standard of living — the way people spend their money, and in public behavior. (1962, pp. 661-62)

Myrdal in *An American Dilemma* also used the criteria of striving and general standards of behavior, rather than delineating occupational and income requirements for middle-class status (1964, p. 704). Finally, Nathan Hare dealt only in purely descriptive terms of behavior and attitude, saying that socioeconomic position was not germane to an analysis of the black Anglo-Saxons (1965, p. 15).

We must take a position contrary to these writers and state that, given any of their criteria as well as others which we shall develop, the blue-collar, stably-employed black man is sufficiently different from the white-collar so as not to be considered middle class. Rather, blue-collar blacks should be viewed as a distinct entity, not middle class and also not lower class, a term which we shall reserve for the unstable, poverty-stricken, unemployed or sporadically employed, bottom strata of the black population. Perhaps a good term for the blue-collar group would be working class.

Our case for this class distinction rests on a number of theoretical bases. Max Weber, in his discussion of the determinants of class-situation, set down three criteria based on market-situation.

> We may speak of a "class" when (1) a number of people have in common a specific causal component of their life chances, in so far as (2) this component is represented exclusively by economic interests in the possession of goods and opportunities for income, and (3) is represented under the conditions of the commodity or labor markets. (1946, p. 181)

These determinants are somewhat in line with Frazier's definition, but going beyond these one can add the additional criteria of collectivities as "people who have a sense of solidarity by virtue of sharing common values and who have acquired an attendant sense of moral obligation to fulfill role-expectations" (Merton 1957, p. 299). This sense of values and role expectations reflects Drake and Cayton and Myrdal's position. The combination of these criteria, socioeconomic and shared value-orientations, with a third, namely, class consciousness — a term which we will take only in the singular sense of class identification and not in the rigorous sense in which Ossowski (1966, p. 92) uses it — gives a definition with more rigor than has been used in the past and one with which we will show that there are major differences between the blue-collar and white-collar groups in the black population.

This problem of class differences is especially acute if one prescribes to the position taken by Wilensky and Lebeaux:

The lines between the upper-working class and the lower-middle class — between the mass of foremen, craftsmen, and high-paid operatives, on the one hand, and the mass of clerks, salesmen, small entrepreneurs, managers with a few subordinates, semi-professionals, semi-technical people, on the other — these are blurring. (1965, pp. XXVI-XXVII)

The problem was fully developed and discussed by Lasswell many years ago:

The lesser middle-class is composed of those who exercise skills which are requited by modest money returns. Hence the class comprises small farmers, small businessmen, low-salaried professional people, skilled workers and craftsmen. The manual workers are those who have acquired little skill; they are the true proletariat. The line between plutocracy, lesser bourgeoisie, and proletariat is a matter of acrimonious debate in practical politics, and of great uncertainty among scientists. (1936, p. 17)

Yet we feel that there are meaningful differences between the blue-collar and white-collar segments of the black population that can be observed. Therefore, we will test this proposition over the eight areas of socioeconomic status, family life, religion, consumption patterns, political participation, inter- and intraracial feelings, and personality characteristics. We will do this by utilizing the sample of blue-collar, stably-employed blacks described in Chapter 1.

The first clue to the differences between these groups is given by their class identifications. As the data in Table 3.1 shows, the blue-collar

TABLE 3.1
PERCENT DISTRIBUTION OF
CLASS IDENTIFICATION BY OCCUPATION

	White-Collar	Blue-Collar
Upper class	2%	5%
Middle class	55	20
Working class	38	75
Lower class	—	—
Would not class himself	5	—
TOTAL	100%	100%
N =	(60)	(20)

blacks overwhelmingly identify with the working class and do not perceive themselves as bourgeoisie. The majority of the white-collar group do identify themselves as middle class, but a significant proportion, almost 40 percent, also perceive themselves as working class. Therefore we do have a blurring of class lines, but the identifications for each group as a whole are clearly different. It is interesting to note that two individuals, one from each group, identify themselves as upper class. One, a physician with a personal income of over twenty thousand dollars per year, and of Haitian background, can perhaps rightly be considered upper class, but the other is a machine operator who earns $7,000 per year, lives in his own house, but does not even own an automobile or any other consumption items which could give him feelings of grandeur. He is the son of a Kentucky coal miner, however, so perhaps relative to the position of his father, he feels upper class.

Socioeconomic Status

We know that these groups of blacks are occupationally different, whether we classify them as white-collar, blue-collar, non-manual, or manual. In terms of income they also differ considerably. The median personal income of the white-collar group is approximately $9,000 per year as compared to only $6,000 for the blue-collar group. In terms of family income the gap is even wider, with the white-collar group earning a median income of approximately $15,000 per year as compared to only $8,000 for the manual workers.

Educationally, also, these groups differ considerably. Of the white-collar group, almost two-thirds hold college degrees; of the blue-collar workers, only 5 percent (or one person) can claim a college degree, and two-fifths have not graduated from high school. Since wives can influence the life style of a family as much as husbands, we also investigated their educational background and again the difference between groups is apparent. Over half of the white-collar wives have graduated from college, and an additional 35 percent have had some college experience. For the blue-collar group, approximately one-third of the wives have had some college training, but only one has received a degree.

In conclusion, we can say that the blue-collar workers hold less prestigious jobs, have less education, and earn much less income than the white-collar workers. Thus, in terms of their market-determined class situation, these groups are quite different.

Family Patterns

The one area of social life in which the blue-collar workers correspond most closely to the white-collar group is that of family patterns. Both groups report about the same proportion of marital dissolution, about 20 percent. They also show similar patterns of fertility, with three-fourths of both groups having two children or less. Their color preferences for females are also similar. Two-fifths of both groups married females of the same color shade as themselves and two-fifths married lighter-colored females. Only one-fifth of both groups married women of a darker shade than themselves, indicating that the preference for lighter-colored females is prevalent for both the white-collar and the blue-collar strata.

Religion

Religion is practiced differently by the lower class than the middle class. To the lower class, religion is a very expressive and emotion-laden activity, characterized by individuals "flailing their arms about, crying, running up and down aisles, yelling *Amen* and Hallelujah" (Drake and Cayton 1962, p. 621). For the middle class it is more staid, and instead of stirring emotions, the quality of the classic religious music and the sober message given by the minister gives the congregation a very orderly and subdued appearance. The fundamentalist expressive behavior is attributable to Baptist affiliation especially, and also to Methodist (Drake and Cayton 1962, p. 621). Looking at the religious affiliation of these groups (Table 3.2), we see that the blue-collar group fits more closely to the lower-class description.

These data show that the blue-collar workers do have a much higher frequency of Baptist affiliation (lower status) and a much lower frequency of Catholic affiliation (higher status). It is interesting that one white-collar worker claims Muslim affiliation, which is usually associated with the lower class (Essien-Udom 1962, pp. 201-12; Lincoln 1961, pp. 48-49). However, this person cannot be considered a "good Muslim," as he drinks alcoholic beverages and goes to parties, which is taboo behavior for the Black Muslims.

Overall, the blue-collar group does not have the status in religious affiliation that would characterize them as middle class, yet some element of "middle-classness" is present. One out of every five members of the white-collar group had changed religion and the majority had changed

TABLE 3.2

Percent Distribution of Religious
Affiliation by Occupation

	White-Collar	Blue-Collar
Catholic	18%	5%
Methodist	13	10
Episcopalian	7	5
Baptist	13	45
Congregationalist	5	5
Presbyterian	7	10
Protestant, no denomination	8	—
Muslim	2	—
Jehovah's Witness	—	5
No affiliation	27	15
TOTAL	100%	100%
N =	(60)	(20)

from Baptist to some higher status religion. This is also the case for the blue-collar group, as twenty percent have changed religion, and in every case it was a change from Baptist to some higher status religion. The reasons for the changes were the same as for the white-collar group; namely it was the religion of the wife. The male married up in status and changed to the higher status religion of the wife. In one case, however, the change was prompted by another middle-class aspiration, that of providing a good education for their children. A forty-nine-year-old pullman porter changed his religion from Baptist to Catholic because of the:

> "co-operation of parochial teachers and school officials that you can't receive as a black from the public school." (Case No. 77)

In general, however, the blue-collar segment does not have the middle-class religious affiliation that the white-collar group does. In addition to the differences in type of affiliation, there is also a difference in the percentages reporting no religion. If one wants to describe lack of affiliation as a rational secularizing trait, then the white-collar group must be considered more secular, with over 25 percent reporting no religion as compared to 15 percent of the blue-collar group.

Consumption Patterns

Students of race relations and class structure define middle-class status in terms of standard of living and life style. Life style and standard of living can be operationalized by measures of consumption. Our expectation is that although there may be many similarities between white- and blue-collar workers in this area, there should be major differences that stem from the different educational backgrounds of these groups.

Considering consumptive behavior, the blue-collar does, in fact, present an element of striving. A comparison of the credit purchasing and saving patterns of the two groups evidenced no appreciable difference. The blue-collar group's consumption of mass media in newspaper reading, radio listening, and television viewing was also similar to that of the white-collar group. However, the element of educational differences, we would argue, does assert itself in the differing magazine reading habits of these two groups (Table 3.3).

TABLE 3.3
PERCENT DISTRIBUTION OF TYPES OF MAGAZINES
READ REGULARLY BY OCCUPATION[a]

	White-Collar	Blue-Collar
None	5%	40%
Sports	3	15
News	80	40
Family	17	25
Male (White)	25	10
Black (Ebony, Jet)	63	55
Technical and professional	32	5
N=	(60)	(20)

[a]Percentages add up to more than 100 because of multiple response.

It is apparent that the blue-collar group reads less magazines than the white-collar group; two-fifths of them read none as compared to only 5 percent of the white-collar group. In addition to the difference in frequency, there is also quite a difference by type. Four out of five persons in the white-collar category read news magazines regularly in contrast to only two out of five in the blue-collar group. Also, almost one-third of the white-collar group read technical and professional journals compared to only one person doing so in the blue-collar group.

The difference in educational background can also be seen in the differential participation in cultural activities of these groups. These data (Table 3.4) show that in no area does the blue-collar group compare favorably with the white-collar except perhaps in the attendance of jazz concerts.

We investigated the two major expensive items of consumption, housing and transportation, and found no apparent differences in terms of size of dwelling unit or in number and type of automobile(s) between the groups. Even though there were no observed differences, it can be argued that there is one in the sense that the blue-collar workers must be spending a greater proportion of their incomes for these items than the

TABLE 3.4

PERCENT DISTRIBUTION OF PARTICIPATION IN
CULTURAL ACTIVITIES (MORE THAN ONCE OR
TWICE PER YEAR) BY OCCUPATION[a]

	White-Collar	Blue-Collar
Classical music concerts	45%	10%
Jazz concerts	60	50
Legitimate theater	83	35
Lectures	52	40
Museums	73	45
Reading books	88	45
N=	(60)	(20)

[a]Percentages add up to more than 100 because of multiple response.

white-collar group since we know that there is a mean family income gap of $7,000 per year between these groups.

Finally, these groups responded similarly for the specific item of drinking behavior and for leisure time activities in general. It appears that the blue-collar group is slightly less "respectable" than the white, as 35 percent of them report engaging in the activities of nightclubbing, partying, and playing cards once a week or more as compared to one-fourth of the white.

In sum, although there is a good deal of similarity between these groups in terms of consumptive behavior, differences are evident and based in part upon the lower educational and income levels of the blue-collar workers.

Political Attitudes and Participation

The primary emphasis of this section will be on the degree of acquiescence to the Democratic political organization evidenced by the blue-collar group. As the data presented in Chapter 2 indicates, white-collar, middle-class blacks express a great deal of independence of the Chicago

Democratic political organization. As a group, they were verbally quite critical of the Daley machine, and they reacted to it by voting independently, splitting their tickets, and supporting machine-opposing candidates for public office. In contrast, the black lower class is almost completely controlled and dominated by the Democratic political interest, as evidenced by high voter turnout and a high degree of straight-ticket Democratic voting (Wilson 1960, pp. 21-77).

A primary aspect of the politics of an individual is his party affiliation. As we indicated in Chapter 2, the white-collar group has moved away from the domination of the Democratic party with less than half of them reporting Democratic affiliation. This is not true for the blue-collar individuals as four out of every five claimed affiliation with the Democrats. In terms of interest in politics and voting, both groups appear to take their citizenship seriously, with over 90 percent of each group reporting that they voted in the 1964 elections and over 80 percent of each group professing high interest in the 1964 campaigns. Although the professed interest and voting turnout of the two groups are similar, from the differences in affiliation we would expect very different voting patterns (Table 3.5).

TABLE 3.5

PERCENT DISTRIBUTION OF VOTING PREFERENCES IN
THE 1964 ELECTIONS BY OCCUPATION

	White-Collar	Blue-Collar
Straight ticket, Democratic	23%	65%
Straight ticket, Republican	—	—
Split ticket, mostly Democratic	60	15
Split ticket, mostly Republican	—	5
Independent	12	5
Did not vote	5	10
TOTAL	100%	100%
N =	(60)	(20)

It is apparent that the majority of the blue-collar workers have succumbed to the Democratic party's influence, as almost two-thirds of them voted the straight Democratic party ticket and only one person voted strictly independent. Their opinions of the Daley machine and of Congressman Dawson, the machine's black representative, were more positive than those of the white-collar group (see Table 3.6).

TABLE 3.6

PERCENT DISTRIBUTION OF OPINIONS OF THE DALEY MACHINE
AND CONGRESSMAN DAWSON BY OCCUPATION

| | Daley Machine | | William Dawson | |
	White-Collar	Blue-Collar	White-Collar	Blue-Collar
Positive	10%	20%	12%	20%
Ambivalent	7	15	15	5
Negative	80	45	69	50
No information	3	20	5	25
TOTAL	100%	100%	100%	100%
N=	(60)	(60)	(60)	(60)

These results show that the blue-collar group holds slightly more favorable attitudes toward Dawson and the Daley machine, but even more significant is the large percentage who refused to comment on either item. It is difficult to interpret why one-fifth of the respondents would not comment on Daley or Dawson; but a tenable explanation would be that since both Daley and Dawson have come under intense verbal attack during the civil rights movement for lack of response to the black people, a black man who had voted for them would experience considerable dissonance and as a consequence would refuse to comment on them.

In general, even those among the blue-collar workers who felt negatively toward Daley and Dawson were not as intense in their feelings as the white-collar group members whose verbal comments we presented in Chapter 2. Consider the following negative comments about Congressman Dawson, which are typical of all but two of the blue-collar workers who were intensely disgusted with him.

> I think we need some new blood to go along with the New Breed because we are a new breed of people.

> I don't think much of Dawson because to me he is just part of the Daley machine.

Those who felt positively inclined toward Daley are interesting, for some hold this feeling even though they are fully cognizant of the implications of machine control and of the alleged anti-Negro prejudice within it.

I think it's (the Daley machine) impregnable at the present time. I think it is a good thing. I base my opinion on the things Daley has accomplished since he has been in office; the neighborhoods improved and the inner-city improved. I think he has helped the Negroes.

It's got everything all tied up. It's good for the Negro. Other administrations got rid of all the Negroes in city hall; Mayor Daley put them back.

I think he (Mayor Daley) is a capable and able mayor for a city the size of Chicago. He has made tremendous progress. I am not saying that he is not prejudiced because I'm sure that he is, but I'm speaking of the good he has done for the city as a whole.

I don't know, but as far as I'm concerned, it's (the Daley machine) pretty fair. I don't know anything about what Daley has done. I suppose he is a little prejudiced, but the Negroes who have jobs because of his machine still vote for him.

Finally in the realm of political action, one can include the participation in civic and political voluntary organizations as indicative of political interest and sophistication. Here, also, the blue-collar workers are not nearly as closely allied with the white-collar group. Fully 80 percent of the blue-collar group do not belong to or attend any voluntary organizations as compared to only 22 percent of the white. And, of the four individuals that do hold memberships in organizations, all hold them in social and religious organizations, not in civic or political clubs, with one member belonging to a labor union, whereas 40 percent of the white-collar group belong to and attend civic and political organizations.

Perhaps more significant is the fact that in the very important area of civil rights, one-half of the blue-collar group does not participate in any way. Even more striking is the finding that of the ten people who have done something, nine have limited their involvement to only sending money. The lone individual who did actively participate did so in Cleveland before moving to Chicago and has not resumed any sort of participation since coming here. Contrast this to the finding that fully three-fourths of the white-collar group have done something, counting the contribution of money, and 40 percent have engaged in physical activity, and it is evident that the blue-collar group comes off a poor second best in the realm of politics and civil rights.

Intraracial Attitudes

Although Frazier made much of the point that the black bourgeoisie is self-hating and holds strong feelings of race disparagement, the results of the Cornell group's study clearly indicate that group identification is lower and race disparagement higher among lower status individuals (Noel 1964, p. 81). The measures used to determine social status, namely, occupation and education, were delineated such that a high school diploma was considered "high education" and skilled and semi-skilled workers were considered as holding "medium" occupations. However, on the basis of their study and with the differing methods of classification in mind, we would predict that the blue-collar group would be more disparaging of their race and feel less group identification than the white-collar segment.

The first item compared was the mean group score in the anti-black index which is a general measure of intraracial attitude (see Appendix B). The mean score for the white-collar group was 10.1 and for the blue-collar, 11.1, or one point higher. This does not indicate a very large difference, and on the basis of this comparison we can only say that the blue-collar group is only slightly more disparaging of the black race.

In order to gain a finer distinction of intraracial feelings, we asked two seperate questions that required the respondent to make a class distinction. One question asked for an opinion about the black lower class and the other, for an opinion about the black middle class. Table 3.7 presents the distribution of responses to these two questions.

This tabulation clearly shows that there is no real difference in attitude toward the middle class between these groups. Approximately

TABLE 3.7

PERCENT DISTRIBUTION OF OPINIONS TOWARD THE MIDDLE
CLASS AND THE LOWER CLASS BY OCCUPATION

| | Toward the Middle Class | | Toward the Lower Class | |
	White-Collar	Blue-Collar	White-Collar	Blue-Collar
Positive	36%	40%	63%	80%
Ambiguous	15	20	10	10
Negative	44	35	22	10
No information	5	5	5	—
TOTAL	100%	100%	100%	100%
N=	(16)	(20)	(60)	(20)

two-fifths of both groups hold positive feelings toward the middle class and the same proportion hold negative feelings. The attitudes toward the lower class are congruent also. Both groups are highly positive toward the lower class.

Thus far, the sentiments toward blacks in general and toward particular class distinctions indicate a positive feeling but no evidence of black chauvinism. In order to investigate more fully any chauvinistic expression among these groups, we looked at three items which can be seen as measures of whether or not an individual has any proclivities toward racial closure. The items consisted of questions asking the respondent if he would rather work for a black or white company and what racial mixture he would desire in his residential community and at his place of work. Nationally, Brink and Harris reported that over three-fourths of the blacks they sampled felt that it made no difference what color individual ran the company they worked for (Brink and Harris 1964, p. 236). For the two groups under comparison, the results were similar. Seventy-three percent of the white-collar group and 70 percent of the blue said that it made no difference what color person ran the company. Similar proportions were evidenced in response to the question asking what racial mixture was desirable in the work situation, with 63 percent of the white and 70 percent of the blue-collar group saying that it made no difference. One-fourth of each group would prefer to work in a half-and-half or mostly all-white work setting in order to create greater racial understanding and to learn job practices from whites.

In the realm of residential racial mixture, the proportion of both groups who feel indifferently falls to 50 percent, and the proportion who desire at least a 50 percent white composition rises to one-third. One of the major reasons given was the same as in the case of interracial mixing at work, namely, to increase racial understanding. However, a second primary reason was that respondents felt that community services would be better if a substantial proportion of whites lived in the neighborhood.

Two additional aspects which were measured in regard to racial chauvinism were militancy and attitudes toward African heritage. Since the blue-collar segment appeared much less active in the area of civil rights, it would seem consistent that they evidence a lower degree of militancy than the white-collar group. Yet for the white-collar group it should be remembered that those who felt most militant were not those who participated most. The same is true, it seems, in this instance also, for there is no difference in the mean militancy scores between these groups while there is a substantial difference in their civil rights participation.

The role played by African heritage is an extremely problematic component of the black American's self-identity. The black man was not born in the system of slavery of the rural South but was forcibly transported there from Africa. For a long time this African heritage was a source of stigma for blacks. Sub-Saharan Africa was pictured for a long time as a continent of uncivilized people. It has only been within the last two decades that systematic and professional exploration of African history has uncovered civilizations of high cultural attainment which would give the black American a sense of pride in his ancestry (Curtin 1968, p. 12). Also, it has been only during this period that the rise of African nationalism could provide a source of pride to black people by the emergence of more than thirty new nations.

It is often contended that pride in African heritage is an integral part of the New Negro Creed, paralleling its role as the basis of positive self-identity for the Black Nationalist groups such as the Black Muslims (Essien-Udom 1962; Lincoln 1961). Yet, one author argues that African heritage is a source of shame as well as pride, for the successes of the African nations in achieving independence must be seen in the light of the failure of black Americans to achieve their freedom from a racially discriminating dominant white majority in the United States (Killian 1968, p. 137). Therefore, African independence is a two-edged sword — cutting one pattern of black freedom from white oppressors in Africa and another pattern of the persistence of white domination of blacks in America.

However, the fact remains that now, through the discovery of past civilizations and the present efforts made by Africans for self-determination, there is a much stronger basis for African identity for black people everywhere than there was in the past. So we have a situation where African heritage has been a source of stigma for blacks in the past, but now it provides a stronger basis for cultural identification, although an ambiguous one. Given these conditions, we can expect differences between the white-collar and blue-collar groups on their attitudes toward Africa due mainly to differences in levels of educational attainment. We would expect that the blue-collar group who read less and have lower levels of interest in culture will still feel highly negative toward their African heritage.

The white-collar group is more likely to have greater knowledge and information about past and present African societies; hence they should feel more ambiguous about Africa than the blue-collar workers (Ginsberg 1967). These arguments are clearly born out by the data. Only one in five members of both the blue- and white-collar groups saw African heritage as an advantage. Ambiguity in the sense that the individual could not see African heritage as either an advantage or a disadvantage was most pronounced in the white-collar group where fully half of the members expressed ambiguity as compared to only 15 percent of the blue. Finally, the blue-collar workers were much more negative, as two-thirds of them gave the opinion that African ancestry was a disadvantage compared to less than one-third of the white-collar group. Not only does the blue-collar group feel more negatively toward African ancestry in a quantitative sense, but they also have more intense qualitative sentiments. For example, both groups mentioned the stigma of slavery and culture loss experienced by the black people as well as the stigma associated with black pigmentation, but only among the blue-collar group was the term "savage" used implying a state of bestiality.

> Disadvantage. We are black and black and savage seem to be identical in the minds of the white man.

> Disadvantage. Whenever a Negro tries to do or become something, prejudiced people always throw it in his face that he belongs in Africa, almost as though he were still a savage.

The epitome of denial is evidenced by a thirty-two-year-old body and fender repairman who responded, "Disadvantage. I'm not an African, I'm an American."

To summarize briefly the comparison of intraracial sentiments of the white-collar and the blue-collar groups, it seems consistent over many measures, with the one exception of the pronounced negative attitude toward African ancestry held by the blue-collar group, that the manual-laboring segment does not differ significantly from the white-collar workers and both are generally positively disposed toward the black race.

Interracial Attitudes

The studies that have investigated the interracial attitudes of blacks, or black attitudes toward whites by social class, are consistent in that they show that the lower-class black man evidences higher anti-white feelings than the middle-class black (Williams 1964, p. 260; Westie and Howard 1954). From our investigation of both groups' desires to work for or with whites, and to live with whites, no differences appeared between them. Yet this does not mean that both groups feel the same about whites, as there are other aspects of this dimension to be considered. Although there was only a slight difference between these groups on the anti-black index, there is a larger one on the anti-white index. The mean anti-white score for the white-collar workers is 12.2, but for the blue-collar group it is 13.8. This significant difference indicates that as a whole, the blue-collar blacks do harbor greater feelings of anti-white sentiment.

In order to gain greater depth along this dimension, we asked the respondents if they ever felt hostility toward particular whites or whites in general. The results show that as a whole, the blue-collar group feels slightly more hostile toward whites than the white-collar group does, but even more interesting, their hostility is more of a general nature focusing on whites as a group rather than on any specific persons. For the white-collar group, specific hostility was felt most toward co-workers and secondly toward whites in sales and service positions. This is not the case for the blue-collar group. Since the apparent difference between these groups is one of kind, specific versus general hostility, the explanation could lie in the amount and intensity of interracial contact between these groups. The logical hypothesis would be that those who have contact with specific whites would be more prone to hold hostility toward a particular individual and that those who have less interpersonal contact would hold more general feelings of anti-white hostility.

The comparison of interracial contact in Table 3.8 supports the contention that the group with the higher interpersonal contact, namely the white-collar workers, holds higher specific anti-white feelings, and the blue-collar workers, who have only minimal contact outside the work sphere, feel the greatest amount of generalized anti-white hostility.

A significant question that can be asked is whether the type of hostility, general or specific, has any impact on the desirability to have more contact with whites. From our data it is fairly clear that it does not, as three-fourths of each group do not desire more contact. For both groups the prime area of desirability is social with the creation of greater racial understanding as the reason given.

Since our investigation thus far has shown that the blue-collar group is the most hostile toward whites, we expected that these people had experienced more racial discrimination by whites than the white-collar group. Implied here is a simple model of discrimination producing hostility where individuals who perceive the greatest amount of discrimination directed toward them by whites will react by being more hostile toward whites than others who perceive less discrimination directed toward them. This pattern of reaction to discrimination is born out by our respondents as the blue-collar group saw themselves as "held down" by whites much more than the white-collar group.

TABLE 3.8

PERCENT DISTRIBUTION OF INTERRACIAL CONTACT IN
THE HOME, AT PLACE OF WORK, AT PARTIES, IN
VOLUNTARY ORGANIZATIONS, AND WHILE
IN SCHOOL BY OCCUPATION

	White-Collar (N=60)	Blue-Collar (N=20)
Contact in the home		
None	38%	75%
Some	62	25
TOTAL	100%	100%
Contact at work		
None	2%	—%
Some	98	100%
TOTAL	100%	100%
Contact at parties		
None	17%	70%
Some	83	30
TOTAL	100%	100%
Contact in voluntary organizations		
None	38%	95%
Some	59	5
No information	3	—
TOTAL	100%	100%
Contact while in school		
None	22%	65%
Some	78	35
TOTAL	100%	100%

In order to illustrate the differing configurations of background characteristics, interracial contacts, and perceived discrimination, and to see their effects on an individual's outlook on life, we will present two cases of individuals who feel discrimination has affected them greatly. Both of these cases concern blue-collar workers.

The first respondent is a forty-two-year-old bus driver, who was born and raised in Chicago. He is married and has five children, all in public school. He lives in, and owns, an apartment building with racially mixed tenants. Educationally, he has completed one year of college training in Chicago, and he has contact with whites once a month or more in every area except voluntary organizations of which he belongs to none.

Contact With Whites

This is enough. I work with them, I have white tenants in my building and I come in contact with them socially. So I can't think of any other area I could have or want contact with them.

Hostility Toward Whites

Yes to all whites. Who doesn't?

Under What Circumstances

On the job, walking down the street, in the military service. I feel hostile every time I think of how they have deprived me of my freedom and rights.

Relief of Hostility

I have fought in any way and every way that I could to keep them from depriving me of what is rightfully mine. I have fought them physically.

Experiences of Discrimination

When I was trying to buy my first house (at age 25) I had some very hectic experiences with the real estates and the banks, simply because I was a Negro.

Effect on Life

They have kept me from advancing as rapidly as I could have because in spite of the fact that I only have a high school education, I have drive and determination. My forefathers helped to build this country into what it is and I am determined to own a little bit of it.

The second respondent is a forty-nine-year-old janitor who was born and raised in Atlanta, Georgia. He is divorced and has one son, age twenty. He lives in a two-flat apartment which he owns, collecting rent from the other flat. He only completed the eighth grade in Atlanta, and the only contact he has with whites is at work every day.

CONTACT WITH WHITES

This is plenty for me. I don't care about being around them. I know I have to be around them at work. White people are rotten. They will grin in your face and call you a dirty name at the same time. They are ignorant and full of hatred.

HOSTILITY TOWARD WHITES

Yes, toward them all. Not just one, but all of them.

UNDER WHAT CIRCUMSTANCES

Mostly in the civil rights issues. It's burning me up to see how stupid and nasty white people are acting. At one time I was out of work because the place I was working at went out of business, and I went to at least fifty different places where I know they needed help and were hiring white guys and I couldn't get a job. That makes me mad with all of them.

RELIEF OF HOSTILITY

I call them a sack of dirty names.

EXPERIENCES OF DISCRIMINATION

Jobs and in housing. I have been discriminated against, yes. Even when I was in school the Negro had the worst.

EFFECT ON LIFE

My life has been very difficult because of those experiences.

To say that human behavior is complex is an understatement, and to delineate completely the configurations affecting anti-white feelings among black Americans is an infinite task; but it can be seen in these two cases that the Northern-raised black as well as the Southern-raised has personally felt the disadvantage of being black. One has fought whites physically; the other called them dirty names. Both care for no more contact with them, and both, having little education, have had to work in manual labor all of their lives and every day must deal with white people, for whom they profess no liking. Each has achieved propertied status in Chicago. Do they label themselves middle class? The two cases we presented do not. Even though they are property owners, they identified themselves as working class.

We can conclude that in the area of interracial sentiments, the blue-collar workers feel more hostile toward whites in general than the white-collar group. This feeling stems from fewer interracial contacts and a higher amount of perceived discrimination.

Personality Characteristics

The two personality measures that we have are indexes of conformity and authoritarianism (see Appendix B). In addition, there is the measure of anti-Semitism which is highly correlated with authoritarianism. Given the greatly differing educational levels of these two groups and the relationships that these items have to education, we can predict that the blue-collar group will significantly differ from the white-collar on these items. This prediction is born out by the data. The blue-collar group scored much higher on the conformity index than the white, with the mean for the blue-collar group being 16.8 and for the white, 14.6. An even more striking difference is found on the authoritarian index, where the mean score for the white-collar group is 17.9 and jumps to 21.4 for the blue. It is not surprising then, with the blue-collar workers being authoritarian and conformist, that they are also more anti-Semitic. Sixty percent of them scored high on the anti-Semitism index compared to 47 percent for the white-collar group. These findings of higher authoritarianism, conformity, and anti-Semitism on the part of working-class blacks are consistent with other research findings (Simpson 1959, pp. 138-46).

Conclusions

In this chapter we have attempted to draw a comparison between the white-collar group and the stably-employed blue-collar black to see if the blue-collar segment is truly part of the black middle class or if it should be viewed analytically as a separate entity. In the strictest sense of occupational, educational, and income lines of demarcation, the blue-collar group falls far below that of the white-collar group. As a consequence of these differences, there are major disparities between these groups in certain areas, such as cultural style of life, although not in the consumption of durable goods. The family patterns of the two groups are very similar, but their religious patterns are quite different, with the blue-collar group showing the same characteristics in this area as the lower class. Differences in political life, inter- and intraracial sentiments, and personality characteristics are easily traceable to inferior education, lack of sophistication, and less integration with the white community rather than to any intrinsic ideological position. In short, there are meaningful differences between the blue-collar and the white-collar black man. Therefore, we would argue that the blue-collar group should be classed apart from the middle class and conceptualized as a different category, different from the middle class and distinct from the lower class.

Although we would separate this group from the middle class, we do feel, however, that probably they are much closer to the middle class than to the lower class in the areas of market situation, shared value orientations, and class identification. One has but to compare these data with the lucid descriptions of the lower class given by others (Drake and Cayton 1962, pp. 563-658; Moynihan 1965; Caplovitz 1963; Moore 1969) to see that just the fact that the blue-collar individuals in our sample were stably employed sets them far apart from the lower-class blacks with their insecure economic position, lack of primary group ties, large families, and almost total lack of the many rewards and gratifications that American society has to offer.

4

Analytic Types
within the
Black Middle Class

The literature describing black people in American society abounds with the use of types and typologies. Basically, there are two methods by which typologies are developed. The first method is based on the individual's or actor's definition of persons in his community and is known as a "social type." The second is based on an observer's or investigator's categorizations and is known as an "analytic type." Although we will treat them separately, it is logically apparent and empirically evident that in many instances they can be and are used in conjunction.

Social types or social typologies based upon individual social characteristics are phenomena independent of the observer. These types, developed from the actor's definition, have many bases. Samuel Strong notes the term "Axes of Life" which encompasses race pride, black-white relations, success, social status, color differentiation, religion, cults and magic, sporting life, and radicalism as the dimensions over which blacks categorize one another into social types (Strong 1962).

Analytic types, like social types, can be based on social characteristics or personality traits, but these categorizations are made by an observer or investigator rather than by the actors themselves. In this respect they are constructs for analysis developed by the investigator to aid him in his understanding of a particular phenomenon, as opposed to social types which are categorizations made by individuals to guide their actions in everyday life.

Analytic typing by personality traits is a very common construct used by psychologists and sociologists alike. For example, in a population we could speak of an authoritarian personality, or cast a person with a proclivity towards prejudice, as a prejudiced personality. Gordon Allport, in investigating personality types among minority groups, persuasively argues for personality types based upon ego defense behavior (Allport 1954, pp. 38-57). He takes his lead from Rosenzweig who argues that reactions to frustration can take three alternative courses in expression: intropunitive, impunitive, and extropunitive (Rosenzweig 1945, pp. 23-30). Omitting the impunitive individual who becomes detached and philosophical about life's frustrations and blames no one, Allport builds his typology on the remaining two types. He pictures the intropunitive individual as one who tends to blame himself for his situation or, if not, for the most part takes the responsibility for correcting or adjusting it on himself. The extropunitive individual is one who blames external forces for his situation and places the burden of restitution upon others.

It is clear that these typing operations overlap. The psychologist such as Allport can delineate the intropunitive type of black personality which in many respects would correspond to the black community's self-definition of the "Uncle Tom" or "white man's nigger." If we use another framework, that of our anti-black and anti-white indexes, this type would probably score high on anti-black feelings and low on anti-white feelings. Of primary concern here is not whether the three methods yield congruity, although it can be seen that they do, but whether, regardless of the method used, a configuration of traits and characteristics can be patterned in such a way that certain types of individuals can be identified and the knowledge of these types used in understanding and predicting attitudes and behaviors.

It is our hypothesis that an analytical typology based upon black-white feelings can prove useful in understanding and predicting the attitudes and behavior of the black middle class. We make this statement with some reservation, however. Given the complexities of human behavior, it is very probable that such a typology is useful only to a degree. Inconsistencies or exceptions are bound to appear. Allport himself provides a useful *caveat* in relation to the use of analytical constructs for minority groups:

> The shortcoming of this analysis is that it may leave in our minds a disorderly array of "mechanisms." Every personality is, in fact, a pattern. A single victim of prejudice may display several traits, frequently blending some on the extropunitive side with some on the intropunitive (1954, p. 156).

Analytical Types

The basis for our analytical typology is the responses of the individuals under study to two sets of statements dealing with attitudes toward whites and toward blacks (see Appendix B). Each individual was given a score on each dimension and then was categorized on the basis of his position either above or below the mean for the sample as a whole. In this manner, we were able to categorize each respondent as either "high" or "low" on attitudes toward whites and blacks. Combining both dimensions, we arrived at the following four analytic types:

"Benevolent"   Below the mean on both the anti-black and anti-white indexes

"Uncle Tom"   Below the mean on the anti-white index and above the mean on the anti-black index

"Race Man"   Above the mean on the anti-white index and below the mean on the anti-black index

"World Hater"   Above the mean on both the anti-black and the anti-white indexes

The labels attached to these analytic types are not intended to be taken literally. They are presented as a shorthand method to partially describe and distinguish the individuals under investigation. We would be the first to agree that the Benevolents are not truly benevolent in every sense of the word, just as the Uncle Toms by their very participation in civil rights do not conform particularly well to the individual black person's subjective definition of an Uncle Tom. Along this line of explication, the Race Men are not racists or black nationalists of the pure type and we cannot say with justification that the World Haters do, indeed, hate the world. Nevertheless, these labels do give a bit of the flavor or the tone of these individuals in relation to their interracial and intraracial dispositions.

The first major point and justification for using this dimension as a basis for analysis is that the encompassing framework of racial prejudice in our society makes it virtually impossible for a member of the black race to escape some form of racial discrimination. There is no niche in the United States completely free from the penetration of discrimination. Given this situation, every black person is faced with the reality that it is a white man's world, owned by and operated by and for the benefit of the white man. Even in the most tolerant interracial situations, in which a child can develop physically and mentally with almost no awareness of the stigma attached to colored skin, when the age of puberty arrives and serious intersexual pairing comes into play, race awareness can no longer be avoided and the black adolescent is faced with the feeling that he or she is somehow not acceptable, somehow inferior (see Chapter 6 for a clear example of this).

This feeling of inferiority or unacceptability requires an individual to become personally segmented (Lewis 1958, p. 189) — that is, in addition to playing the expected roles in differing contexts which everyone must do, he must also play different roles in different racial situations. This is not just an occasional occurrence; rather, it is usually a part of everyday living. The intense demands which this situation places on an individual have profound implications for his self-esteem, self-identity, and group identification. How can this externally-prescribed inferiority be overcome? Depending upon their own experiences and particular environmental pressures, individuals can and do vary greatly in their responses to this situation. But one factor is common to all blacks, although in differing degrees: the environment holds some degree of hostility over and above that held for other members of society.

If the environment is perceived as hostile, then the individual is prone to act in such a manner as to elicit hostility from it. In this situation, a circular type of interaction mode is achieved whereby reactions to the environment reinforce a black person's subjectively-defined discrimination which in turn reinforces the environmental reactions to him. In this manner, the self-fulfilling prophecy of hostility and discrimination becomes deeply entrenched, and the "marks of oppression" become permanent (Kardiner and Ovessy 1951, passim).

If we follow Allport and Rosenzweig, we would say that the reactions to this oppression could be centered around an individual's perception of blame, and we would find both intropunitive and extropunitive personality types. In like manner, Karen Horney categorizes reactions in terms of movement toward, against, or away from the oppressor. Preceding Allport, she too perceived a mixing or blending of responses for any given individual.

It is our contention that the four analytic types — Benevolents, Uncle Toms, Race Men, and World Haters — can subsume both the dichotomous typology of intropunitive and extropunitive and the trichotomous typology of moving toward, against, and away from the oppressor, and can give greater precision to these configurations of interracial reactions of blacks.

It can be argued that all three typologies (those of Rosenzweig, Allport, and Horney) should be class related. High anti-white feelings and the expression in terms of Race Men and World Haters, extropunitive individuals, or those moving against or away from the oppressor, predominate among the lower-class black. The separatist and nationalistic sentiment typified in the Black Muslims is based in the lower-class element (Essien-Udom 1962, pp. 201-12). However, recent events in the civil rights movement such as the slogan of Black Power and the new leadership of SNCC and CORE indicate some basis for this sentiment among members of the middle and upper classes. Low anti-white feeling and expression, or repression of anti-white feeling, is generally associated with black middle-class life. Therefore, the Benevolents and the Uncle Toms or the intropunitive individuals who move toward the oppressor should predominate within our sample.

It would seem logical to argue that feelings toward whites and feelings toward blacks are symmetrical, i.e., if a person were high on anti-white feeling then he would be low on anti-black feeling. Empirically, this is not the case, and it can be argued that phenomenologically it should also not be true. If an individual perceives very little discrimination, feels his environment is not very hostile, and has a sound positive relationship with members of his own race, then he may hold positive feelings toward both races. Similarly, if a black man perceives a great deal of discrimination from whites and feels his environment is very hostile, this perception in turn could evoke feelings of self-hate, loss of self-esteem, and loss of respect for his people because they are black and labeled inferior. Then he would harbor intense anti-white and anti-black sentiments simultaneously, as in the case of the World Hater.

By the nature of the method used to delineate the four types, we can test the symmetry of interracial sentiments. If interracial sentiments are indeed symmetrical and we are forcing a dichotomy on our sample along both dimensions, then we should obtain only two groups, namely, Uncle Toms and Race Men (See Table 4.1).

TABLE 4.1

DISTRIBUTION OF ATTITUDE TOWARD WHITES BY
ATTITUDES TOWARD BLACKS

Anti-white Index Score	Anti-black Index Score	Frequency	Percent
Below the mean	Below the mean	19	32
Below the mean	Above the mean	16	27
Above the mean	Below the mean	14	23
Above the mean	Above the mean	11	18
Total		(60)	100%

The results in Table 4.1 indicate that symmetry in interracial attitudes is not the case, as the sample is far from dichotomized. In fact, with exactly one-half of the cases falling in the asymmetrical categories, no statistical test is necessary to back up the assertion that interracial sentiments are not symmetrical.

Demographic and Social Profiles of These Types

Since these dispositions are shaped, formed, and reinforced by background characteristics and experiential phenomena, our primary goal is to attempt to map out the patterns of relationship between these dispositions and relevant personal characteristics. The first area we will sketch out is a demographic and social profile of our four types. Table 4.2 presents this information.

The first and most notable characteristic which distinguishes the Benevolent from the other types is his youth. Over 40 percent of the Benevolents are under the age of thirty and fully two-thirds of them are under forty. Three other characteristics distinguishing this type from at least two of the others are found in the facts that they tend to be government employees, to have lower incomes, and to come from white-collar families. In this last characteristic, occupational stability, they resemble the World Haters, but on practically every other comparison these two types appear the farthest apart.

What assertions can we now make regarding the relationship between the background characteristics of the Benevolents and their seemingly tolerant and accepting interracial attitudes? Perhaps the most justifiable statement is that in large part their positive attitudes toward their own race and toward whites is due to their youth. In a very extensive study of many forms of tolerance and intolerance, Samuel Stouffer found that younger people were much more tolerant than older (1955, p. 220). It is often asserted that one reason for the higher tolerance of youth is their increased educational levels compared to older persons. Since for our sample the Benevolents do have a high level of education but not significantly higher than at least two of the other types, age must have an effect of its own. This assertion is consistent with Robin Williams' finding that even controlling for educational level, the younger age group of blacks was less prejudiced than the older (1964, p. 268).

The other background characteristic which could have a bearing on the interracial outlook of this type is the relatively high level of

TABLE 4.2

PERCENT DISTRIBUTION OF SOCIAL AND DEMOGRAPHIC
CHARACTERISTICS BY ANALYTIC TYPE

	Benevolents (N=19) 100%	Uncle Toms (N=16) 100%	Race Men (N=14) 100%	World Haters (N=11) 100%
Age				
21 to 30 years	42%	6%	21%	9%
31 to 40 years	26	19	36	27
41 years and over	32	75	43	64
Skin shade of male				
Dark brown	26%	25%	36%	18%
Brown	47	56	43	46
Fair or lighter	21	12	21	36
No information	5	6	—	—
Occupation				
Professional or proprietor	21%	44%	43%	46%
Private enterprise employee	32	12	29	27
Governmental employee	47	44	29	27
Education				
Less than high school	—%	6%	7%	9%
Completed high school	5	6	29	—
Some college	32	25	7	9
College graduate	63	62	57	82
Personal income				
Less than $7,000 per year	10%	19%	7%	—%
$7,100 to $9,999	53	25	43	27
$10,000 or more	37	56	50	73
Area raised				
South	47%	50%	7%	54%
Non-South	53	50	93	46
Intergenerational occupational mobility				
Upwardly mobile	53%	81%	71%	54%
Stable or downwardly mobile	42	19	29	46
No information	5	—	—	—
Religious preference				
None	32%	31%	29%	9%
Catholic	10	25	21	18
Other Protestant	42	31	28	64
Baptist	16	12	14	9
Muslim	—	—	7	—

intergenerational occupational stability. According to Bettleheim and Janowitz's thesis, this condition would not be overly conducive to the development of tolerant and accepting attitudes. Yet one can argue that, for
the stable member of a minority group situated at the white-collar level,
occupational stability would have a positive effect on interracial attitudes.
The individual in this instance is socialized into an environment where

his family and very probably the families he interacts with hold quite respectable positions in the community because of their fairly high-status occupational positions. It follows then that he would hold positive feelings toward such people. And it could also logically follow that by the very holding of these status positions in a community dominated by white interests, the individual would not be too negative toward these white interests; hence, he would have positive feelings toward both whites and blacks. However, people are not always logical, nor do they perceive situations in the same way as some naive observer. Therefore, if this argument is valid, how can we explain the connection between the negative interracial sentiments and the concomitant high rate of occupational stability evidenced by the World Haters? We cannot resolve this dilemma with the information given up to this point, but later in this chapter and in the next we will consider additional factors related to this subject.

The first demographic characteristic which distinguishes the Uncle Toms from the Benevolents is age. The former type is older than any of the others, with fully three-fourths of them over the age of forty. They have the highest rate of occupational mobility and the highest proportion of Catholic affiliation (one-fourth). Like the Benevolents, they too have a high proportion in governmental employment.

For Uncle Toms we would contend that the distinguishing characteristics are consistent with their interracial sentiments as well as consistent with each other. In addition, three out of the four characteristics are reflective of Frazier's description of the black bourgeoisie. Their advanced age is consistent with their interracial attitude of acceptance of "the system." We cannot look back in retrospect to see if these attitudes at some earlier point in time were different. However, we can assert that at this point the Uncle Toms' negative attitude toward blacks, positive position toward whites, and high rate of social mobility are indicative of the final stage of persons who have moved toward the oppressor and away from the masses of their own people. They have accepted the system.

Pettigrew notes that intense anti-white attitudes (movement against the oppressor) are associated with lower-status and darker-colored individuals (Pettigrew 1964, p. 40). His reasoning is that lower-status individuals are more prone to use direct action in response to oppression and that darker individuals are forced by their very coloring to identify with the oppressed minority and cannot easily utilize mechanisms to escape this identification. Juxtaposed on these variables is the finding that blacks with Southern experience as a group are more passive and accepting for fear of repressive retaliation (Karon 1958, passim). We would argue that holding high anti-white attitudes is a necessary predisposition for moving against the oppressor, and thus we can predict that the variables of skin color, status, and Southern experience should be related to the analytic types of Race Men and World Haters.

Looking at the Race Men first, we do find a major difference in educational status. The Race Men have the lowest educational attainment of any type, with over one-third not having any college experience. They are also the darkest group in terms of skin color, with over one-third of them falling into the dark brown category. In terms of Southern experience, we find the Race Men have almost none, with only one individual having been raised in the South. Thus, for this type which is most predisposed to moving against the oppressor, we do find the related characteristics that other researchers have found, namely, low education, darker skin coloring, and little Southern experience. In addition, the only Black Muslim found in our sample is a Race Man, a fact which at least symbolically supports the moving-against-the-oppressor attitude of this type.

The World Haters present a very complex problem for analysis in theoretical terms. They have neither a racial nor ethnic identification. Their demographic and social characteristics cast them as older, of lighter color, and more highly educated than any other group. In line with their higher educational attainment is the fact that they have the highest personal income of any group. They also have a high proportion of occupationally stable individuals (46 percent). In general, they have the highest socioeconomic status of any of the four types.

Perhaps the most interesting distinguishing characteristic of this type is their high rate of religious affiliation and identification. Almost one-third of all of the other types claim no religious affiliation, yet only one individual out of the eleven World Haters does not.

On the basis of these findings we would argue that this group can best be characterized as moving away. They are not only moving away from the oppressor who, given the World Haters' high status, cannot have oppressed them too much, but also moving away or withdrawing from society in general. In a sense, they have withdrawn within themselves. Their high degree of religious affiliation is one indication of this, although admittedly crude. These individuals who hold such negative feelings toward not only whites but toward their own people as well must be under constant tensions and strains resulting from the powerful cross-pressures of a negative variety operating in their daily lives. Their very high socioeconomic status, their lack of identification with either whites or blacks, and their high identification with religion certainly separates this type from the others. It is interesting to note the effect of these personal conditions on their attitudes and behaviors which we can measure and comment upon.

Behavioral Concomitants of the Typology

Given the knowledge that we now have about the social background characteristics and the interracial attitudes of these four types, it is possible to make certain predictions regarding their behavior and specific attitudes. One could argue that the behavioral variables which we will look at are perhaps just as important in shaping the interracial attitude dimensions as background characteristics; in fact, some of them could be classified as background characteristics. By our labeling of these variables as "concomitants" rather than effects, we will elude for the moment the issue of cause and effect, in order to present a relational analysis at this point. Later in the concluding chapter we will make our theoretical formulations explicit in light of these relational data, and we will develop a theory of black-white relations, focusing on the black middle class.

For the Benevolents we propose that their behavior will evidence a quality of openness and acceptance of, even altruism toward, both races. If in fact they are living by the American creed of equality and personal worth, then they should evidence little of the behaviors associated with personal stress.

From the information that we have, it appears that these predictions are moderately supported (see Table 4.3). If we add the comparative skin shade of the spouses of this group and keep in mind the cultural desirability of light females within the black community, it is evident that this group, more than any of the others, is willing to marry females darker than themselves, thereby showing the greatest penetration of the idea that "Black is Beautiful." Another behavioral characteristic which is consistent with their position although not too different from the other types is the relatively high contact that they have with whites in their homes.

We hypothesized that the Benevolents would evidence comparatively little stress because of their value orientation. In measuring stress we used the consumption of alcohol and physiological symptoms. Excessive alcohol consumption, it can be argued, is a mechanism of escape from reality and the problems that one faces — in short, a crude indi-

TABLE 4.3

PERCENT DISTRIBUTION OF THE BEHAVIORAL
CONCOMITANTS OF THE TYPOLOGY

	Benevolents (N=19)	Uncle Toms (N=16)	Race Men (N=14)	World Haters (N=11)
Comparative skin color of wife				
Male darker than female	37%	38%	29%	9%
Female darker than male	16	—	7	—
Same skin shade	10	31	21	54
No information	37	31	43	36
Total	100%	100%	100%	100%
Contact with whites in the home				
Some	68%	62%	50%	64%
None	32	38	50	36
Total	100%	100%	100%	100%
Symptoms of stress[a]				
None	32%	19%	7%	—%
One	21	19	21	23
Two or more	47	62	72	77
Total	100%	100%	100%	100%
Alcohol consumption				
None	5%	19%	—%	—%
Drinks moderately, once or twice a week or less	58	56	50	46
Drinks every day but was not high the week before	26	19	21	27
Drinks every day and was high the week before	10	6	29	27
Total	100%	100%	100%	100%
Type of civil rights participation				
None	21%	31%	50%	9%
Contributions only	21	25	29	54
Active participation	58	44	21	37
Total	100%	100%	100%	100%
Participation in fraternal organizations				
None	37%	44%	71%	46%
Past member, not active now	42	31	29	46
Present member, active now	21	25	—	9
Total	100%	100%	100%	100%

[a]See Appendix A, page B of the questionnaire for a listing of these symptoms.

cator of stress. Previous research has shown that middle-class blacks purchase and consume more alcohol than middle-class whites (Stafford,

Cox, and Higgenbotham 1968, p. 91) and they prefer the "high status" or status-conferring liquors; especially Scotch (Bauer 1965, p. 3; Media-scope 1964, p. 77). We could expect, then, that within the black middle class, those members who feel the greatest stress may relieve their tensions through the use of alcohol.

We would also argue that physiological or somatic disturbances can be symptomatic of inner stress. Kardiner and Ovessy state that "a tension can force itself into awareness in some distorted manner, or failing that, may seek physiological discharge like hypertension, gastric spasm, diarrhea, etc." (1951, p. 8).

The Benevolents as a group evidence the least amount of symptoms of stress as compared with other types; almost one-third of them, the highest percentage of any group, reported none. In terms of alcohol consumption this type had one of the lowest percentages of persons who were high during the preceding week.

This group's behavior in the realm of civil rights appears to be consistent with their attitude. Over half of them actively participate in the civil rights movement, a fact which is consistent not only with their feelings about their own people but also with their youth, if we assume youth's proclivity for action. Somewhat incongruent with our prediction is this group's fraternal activity. Frazier and others pictured fraternal organization activity as a status-seeking and status-enhancing activity, one practiced by the black bourgeoisie. Yet for our sample the figures for membership and activity in these organizations of the Benevolents are almost the same as those of the Uncle Toms. The only explanation we can offer is that, given the young age of this group, they are not too far removed from their educational processes and still retain their ties with the educational community through fraternal organizations. Still, only about one-fifth of them have remained active.

The pressures of being a black and holding anti-black attitudes must evidence themselves in some overt manner. The situation of the Uncle Toms by its very nature implies a great deal of role-playing. The high valuation placed on being and acting "white" should manifest itself in some form.

The value of lightness of females is apparent in the Uncle Tom group. In no case is the female darker than the male; this type's preference is for either the same shade or lighter females. Contact with whites in the home is as high as that for any other group, although we might have expected it to be much higher. Also, it must be noted that we investigated the amount of contact with whites in voluntary organizations under the assumption that the Uncle Toms would actively seek inter-racial contact. This assumption was not supported. In terms of stress, this type evidences more physiological symptoms than the Benevolents but less than the other two groups (the Race Men and the World Haters), and they have the lowest incidence of excessive alcohol consumption. One could argue that, if they are attempting to enhance their status and image in the eyes of whites, overindulgence of alcohol would be strictly avoided.

Consistent with the Uncle Toms' status-seeking image is their active participation in fraternal organizations; over 50 percent have been members at one time and one-fourth are still active. Their participation in civil rights is greater than we would expect. However, our general hypothesis was that the civil rights movement would have an impact on the black middle class as a whole, and the high activity of this group could be seen as a manifestation of this.

The behavioral analysis of the next two types, Race Men and World Haters, should prove interesting, for in these types we have minority group members who are manifestly negative in their attitude toward the dominant white majority, and the mechanisms by which these types act out their feelings are not well known.

The Race Men are darkest in skin shade, and therefore marriage to a female of similar coloring does not have the same meaning as for the other three types. Their behavior in this realm is slightly indicative of positive attitudes toward blacks, as half of them marry dark women. However, their contact with whites, although it is the lowest of any type, is still quite high with 50 percent having some contact in their homes. From the measures of stress we have, it is apparent that this group along with the World Haters shows the greatest evidence of tensions and stress. Almost three-fourths of them report two or more symptoms for the week preceding the interview, and almost one-third of them report being high during the same period. It is also noteworthy that none of the Race Men are total abstainers from alcohol. Their participation in fraternal organizations is expectedly low, since this phenomenon is associated with higher education.

Their relatively low participation in civil rights was not predictable. One-half of the Race Men do not now participate nor have they ever participated in civil rights organizations. A possible explanation of this phenomenon is that for some reason Race Men are unable to give expression to their sentiments and instead release their tensions through mechanisms of drinking (withdrawal and escape) and physiological disorders. Perhaps the task seems too great, the barriers insurmountable. Fear that the civil rights goals, no matter how noble, are not realistic may play a part in their limited involvement. Perhaps some of the reasons for this apparent paradox will come to the surface in the case analysis presented later.

Finally, when we consider the World Haters, one of the most dominant characteristics is their light color. Consistent with this is their preference for lighter-colored females. In every case, the wife is either the same shade as the male, or lighter. The amount of contact with whites in the home is about the same as it is in any other group. As we mentioned earlier, the most dramatic evidence of their negative dispositions is their outward manifestations of stress. All of the members of this type evidenced some physiological symptom or symptoms, and comparatively speaking, their consumption of alcohol is high. Their activity in fraternal organizations in minimal. In terms of civil rights participation, the World Haters are the highest monetary contributors, a fact indicative of some sort of detached involvement; yet their active participation is substantial, with over one-third of them donating their physical efforts.

We can conclude from these data that behavior is somewhat consistent with underlying interracial attitudes. Nevertheless, the correspondence is far from perfect, since many other areas were investigated and no differences among groups revealed themselves. This finding indicates that only a low degree of crystallization of behavior with underlying interracial dispositions has been achieved.

Attitudinal Concomitants of the Typology

In this section we will compare some specific attitudes of our four types over the bi-racial dimension (see Table 4.4). Here, as in the previous section, we will be looking for the consistency of specific sentiments with the underlying dispositions toward whites and blacks. Our predictions remain the same for attitudes as they were for behavior.

The Benevolents appear to feel less discrimination than any other group; almost two-thirds of them perceive only some discrimination. The modal effect of discrimination on all four types followed two themes: it made them more realistic about their life chances and it motivated them to work harder. (See Chapter 6 for a detailed account of the effects of discrimination on a black man's life). The dominant response of the Benevolents followed three themes. However, for over one-third of

TABLE 4.4

PERCENT DISTRIBUTION OF THE SPECIFIC ATTITUDINAL
CONCOMITANTS OF THE TYPOLOGY

	Benevolents (N=19)	Uncle Toms (N=16)	Race Men (N=14)	World Haters (N=11)
Perceived discrimination				
Some or very little	63%	44%	57%	54%
A great deal	37	56	43	46
Total	100%	100%	100%	100%
Effect of discrimination on life				
None	16%	19%	—%	18%
Made individual more realistic about life chances or motivated him to work harder	47	44	50	63
Increased hostility toward the white man	37	37	50	18
Total	100%	100%	100%	100%
Militancy index				
Low	47%	75%	29%	63%
High	53	25	71	37
Total	100%	100%	100%	100%
Attitude toward blacks "passing"				
Accepting	26%	44%	29%	27%
Ambivalent	21	37	29	46
Unaccepting	53	19	43	27
Total	100%	100%	100%	100%
Attitude toward lower-class blacks				
Positive	63%	44%	71%	82%
Ambivalent	21	19	7	9
Negative	16	38	21	9
Total	100%	100%	100%	100%
Attitude toward middle-class blacks				
Positive	42%	38%	43%	27%
Ambivalent	5	38	7	18
Negative	53	25	50	55
Total	100%	100%	100%	100%
Attitude toward African heritage				
Positive	16%	12%	43%	18%
Ambivalent	58	50	43	46
Negative	26	38	14	36
Total	100%	100%	100%	100%

them, it raised their level of hostility toward whites from what it had been before they fully realized the extent to which they were suffering from white-directed discrimination. Perhaps reflective of their feelings is the fact that about half of this group scored high on the militancy index. Consistent with their positive feelings toward their race is their negative attitude toward blacks "passing." Slightly more than half of the Benevolents were unable to accept this mode of behavior, the highest percentage of all four types. They are generally positive in their feelings toward lower-class blacks and almost evenly split on their feelings toward the black middle class. Our expectation was that their youth and disposition would also cause them to evidence a high amount of race pride and pride in African heritage. This is not the case, as most are ambivalent about it, and more have a negative attitude (26 percent) than a positive one (16 percent). Taken as a whole, the specific attitudes of the Benevolents are consistent with a positive bi-racial stance but are far from the tolerant, accepting model type that we expected.

Perhaps the most accommodative type on these attitudinal items are the Uncle Toms. Over half of them feel that they have experienced a great deal of racial discrimination, yet this perception of discrimination has not provoked greater hostility toward whites when compared to the other groups.

They are the least militant of any type, a finding which was predictable on the basis of their pro-white attitude and their advanced age. They are the highest accepters of blacks "passing" and the most negatively disposed toward lower-class blacks. In addition, they are the least negatively disposed toward the black middle class. These traits are very consistent with their image. Further, the element of self-hate that Frazier discusses is somewhat revealed in their attitude toward themselves; although they evidence the lowest percentage of negative feelings toward themselves as a class (25 percent), they are not the most positively inclined. Instead, they show the highest rate of ambiguity, almost 40 percent. Since it is the contention of most writers that this type more than any other desires to identify with the white man, it is not surprising that they are the group with the lowest percentage who feel African ancestry is a positive trait and the group with the highest percentage (along with the World Haters) who consider it an undesirable trait.

The Race Men, too, show a very consistent pattern of specific attitudes in relation to their anti-white proclivities. They perceive a moderate amount of discrimination compared to the other types, but more than any other group feel that it has increased their hostility toward the white man. It is not surprising then that their attitudes are the most militant, for we know that they participate only minimally in an active way. They are for the most part unaccepting of blacks "passing" and they are very positively inclined toward the black lower class. They evidence mixed feelings toward the black middle class, mixed not in the sense that they are ambivalent but in the sense that they are almost evenly split on positive and negative feelings. Finally, as we expected, the Race Men as a type are the most positively disposed toward African ancestry, with double the proportion of any other type having positive feelings (43 percent). The term Race Men seems to fit this type very well.

The attitudes of the World Haters were the least predictable of any group because of the general negative cast to their world view, and the knowledge that they are somehow forced to exist in society. However, it was predictable that, compared to the other types, discrimination has motivated them to work harder and provided them with a greater sense of reality of their life chances. We expected them to perceive more discrimination than they reported since they are evenly split on this item. Generally, they are not very militant, but they are the most ambivalent about blacks "passing." An indication that their anti-black sentiment is not as strong as one would believe from the index is the overwhelming percentage (82 percent) who are positively inclined toward the black lower class. This discrepancy can be explained only tentatively. Our feeling is that an anti-black index composed of a series of statements mixed in with many other statements gives a truer indication of a disposition than an open-ended question where it is possible that the respondent is affected by the presence of a black interviewer. Therefore, we would advance the explanation that it would not be in the spirit of the times for World Haters to answer this question negatively and that, given the very high educational level of this type, they would be sophisticated enough to respond accordingly.

Finally, consistent with the World Haters' position is the fact that more than any other type they are critical of the black middle class. In light of our tentative explanation, this attitude is more acceptable to them and is one which can be and is articulated.

General Image of the Types

Now we have the essential elements needed to trace the patterns of interracial sentiment among middle-class blacks. Generally, we can envisage the Benevolent as a young, highly educated man who takes pride in his race. Although he is not overly hostile toward whites, he is not very accepting of them and manifests this feeling in his active participation in civil rights organizations. The Uncle Tom is an older man, one who has been socially mobile and who has accepted the system of white superiority and domination in both attitude and action. The Race Man is a darker, less educated white-collar worker, who has had little Southern experience. He is very pro-black as well as anti-white in his attitudes, but in terms of behavior he acts only minimally to follow through on his convictions and shows considerable evidence of stress and inner tension. The World Hater is older, light-colored, and holds the highest status positions in the black community. He is quite religious, has a low opinion of the black middle class but professes a liking for the lower class. He contributes to civil rights organizations but does little else actively to alleviate his negative feelings toward either whites or blacks. Consequently, he also evidences behaviors which reflect his tensions and stress.

Since we have but a general image of these types, we will postpone the discussion of our typology's utility until after the next chapter in which we will present detailed case analyses of these types. In this manner the reader can gain a greater depth of understanding of the consistencies and inconsistencies of the middle-class black man's intra-racial and interracial dispositions.

5

A Case Analysis
of Analytic Types
within the
Black Middle Class

In this chapter we present the detailed comments of two typical respondents for each of the four types. Following the comments of the two respondents is a brief discussion and analysis of the pattern they present. For the Race Men, we will also present a third respondent who is unique in terms of his late-in-life change in interracial disposition, but is representative of the impact of the civil rights movement on the black middle class in perhaps an atypically intensive manner.

Benevolents

Case No. 13 is a dark brown, thirty-six-year-old insurance agent. He is an only child and was born and raised by both of his parents in a large Eastern city. His father was a carpenter and his mother a housewife. He is married for the first time and his wife works as a clerk for a utility company. They have no children. He studied at an Eastern university for two years but has no degree. He earns approximately $8,000 per year and his wife earns an additional $5,000. Both are Methodists and attend church on the average of two times per month. He is a member of the YMCA, which he does not attend, and an active adult leader in Boy Scouts. He has donated money to the civil rights movement, but has not participated. He has social contact with whites in his home at least once a week and had contact with them every day in school and while he was growing up. Since his business is strictly with black people, he has no contact with whites on the job and reports that he has none at parties or in voluntary organizations.

Is Present Contact Enough

In all areas it's enough. I don't want to be around them any more than they want to be around me. They feel that all Negroes want to do is socialize.

Participation in Unorganized Protest

No, that's for narrow-minded people to do.

Negroes Passing

I feel it's wrong to deny your race or color.

Is African Ancestry an Advantage or a Disadvantage

I don't see that it is either one. This country is made up of people from everywhere, and regardless of where we come from originally, we are still Negroes and proud of it.

Interracial Marriage

A person should marry whomever he wants. This particular question is the basis of the white man's argument in the discrimination and segregation issues today.

Opinion of Middle-Class Negro

We have a tendency to be individualists. We should work together more and try to help our people be creative.

Opinion of Lower-Class Negro

He could try harder and do some things himself in order to better his own conditions and not be solely dependent upon others. He could learn how to vote and get more education.

Can the Lower-Class Negro Rise from the Ghetto

Yes, because they can do some things to help themselves. They are striving for fair employment and better housing. Some are learning how to vote.

The respondent has no preference as to whom he would rather work alongside, but he would rather live in a fifty-fifty racially mixed neighborhood, "because the housing conditions would be better in a mixed neighborhood." He would find no distaste in eating with, dancing with, or having someone in his family marry a white person.

HOSTILITY TOWARD WHITES

Yes, when I read about some of the things they do to Negroes in the South. Every bad habit the Negro has, he got it from the white man. I feel this way toward whites in general, not just one in particular. And, I get mad every time I read the papers or watch television.

RELIEF OF HOSTILITY

Actually, I don't do anything. I send more money to the NAACP.

The respondent feels that he has suffered very little discrimination and that it has affected his life very little. When asked if he thought that the recent gains made in civil rights were due in part to the increased awareness of Northern whites, he replied, "Yes, because the Northern white taught people how to vote and showed them buying power." The respondent takes a drink once a week on the average and reported no symptoms of stress.

Case No. 29 is a fair, twenty-six-year-old professional musician. He was born and raised in Chicago and grew up with two sisters. He was raised by his mother only, as his father was deceased. His mother had completed college and worked as a file clerk to support the family. He is married for the first time and his wife works as a clerk. They have one daughter of pre-school age. He earned an Associate's degree from a junior college after attending classes for two years. He earns $8,000 per year and his wife an additional $5,000. Both are Episcopalians and attend services on the average of three times a month. He does not belong to any voluntary organizations, nor does his wife. He has contact with whites every day at work and had contact every day while in school and while growing up. He interacts with whites in his home about once a month and also at parties. He contributes money to five civil rights organizations and works on the financial committee of the Coordinating Council of Community Organizations.

IS PRESENT CONTACT ENOUGH

Enough, I don't advocate integration as such. I believe that people should be allowed to choose whom they want to associate with. Being colored, I'm more comfortable around colored people and it doesn't have to have anything to do with color. If we had been raised in the same environment, we would be more compatible.

The respondent has not participated in unorganized protest.

NEGROES PASSING

I think they are a disgrace to the race and disrespectable to themselves and that they have a problem. But, personally, I don't hold it against them if that is what they want to do.

IS AFRICAN ANCESTRY AN ADVANTAGE OR A DISADVANTAGE

Neither one. I don't feel like an African. I see no African blood that I know of. In other words, I can't trace my family tree back to the Africans.

INTERRACIAL MARRIAGE

Okay. Race and marriage have nothing to do with each other. Marriage is not based on race but on personal feelings.

OPINION OF MIDDLE-CLASS NEGRO

He feels like he is so far removed from poverty and racial pressure that he is too complacent. He doesn't feel like there is a racial problem because he has been able to get as far ahead as he has, especially in the middle-class neighborhoods where everyone around him is getting ahead or seems to be getting ahead.

OPINION OF LOWER-CLASS NEGRO

They just aren't prepared and in many cases it is not their own fault, although in many cases it is due to racial prejudice. I feel the only way we are going to rectify the lower-class problem is through education.

CAN THE LOWER-CLASS NEGRO RISE FROM THE GHETTO

Yes, because basically I feel that they want the better things in life, too, and they could attain them if they were taught or trained in skills that they would have the ability to learn.

It makes no difference to the respondent whom he works alongside, but he would rather live in an area of mostly blacks, "because I'm more comfortable with my own kind. I've lived with all whites so I know about that." He would find no distaste in eating or dancing with, or having someone in his family marry a white; but he would find it distasteful to go to a party and find it was composed of all whites.[1]

HOSTILITY TOWARD WHITES

I have my mad days. It depends on how I feel when I get up in the morning. If I read in the paper where a group of whites beat up a colored boy for nothing, of course I feel anger.

The respondent feels that he has experienced some discrimination: "When I was in the Air Force and I was in Texas, I was asked out of several theaters. It affected me quite a bit because I had never experienced this before. It affected me this way because I suddenly became aware that this existed." He felt that it had an effect on his life: "It changes your outlook and attitude when you discover that these things really happen. This woke me up to the fact that they were all true."

This respondent takes a drink once or twice a week either at home or at a friend's house and he reported that he had a common cold in the week previous to the interview.

Discussion

Both of these are quite comparable in terms of background. They both are young, are products of a Northern environment, and have fairly high incomes because of their working wives. They do differ in civil rights participation, but both have contact with whites. Neither desires more contact with whites for vanity or any other reason. Neither one has participated in unorganized protest but they do evidence some pride in their race by their negative attitudes toward "passing." It is interesting that Case No. 29 feels that "passing" is disgraceful yet he is not vengeful

---

[1] A social distance scale did not work at all for this study and this case is exemplary. The differing situations are perceived in a different light by many of the respondents so Gutmann scaling or any systematic scoring did not work. Many respondents also indicated that it depended on the individual whether or not it would be distasteful — so scoring was impossible.

toward those who practice it. Neither, although they both evidence some race pride, feels any affinity toward Africa. Both feel that marriage is a personal thing and interracial marriage is up to the individual. Neither could be classed as strongly opposed to either the middle-class or lower-class, but both are generally critical of the middle-class black for not helping the race and of the lower-class black for not helping himself. Coming from a Northern environment neither has experienced much discrimination and their manifestations of hostility toward whites stems mostly from perceiving racial discrimination through the mass media. To relieve these tensions, Case No. 13 sent more money to the NAACP and Case No. 29 evidenced no expressive mechanisms. Neither showed any outward manifestations of intense stress or strain.

Uncle Toms

Case No. 11 is a fair, fifty-four-year-old manager of a clothing store. He was born and raised by both parents in a border state city and had one sister and one brother. His father was a stone mason and his mother a housewife. He is married to his first wife who does not work. They have one daughter who attends a Catholic high school. He completed one year of college at a local university. He earns about $10,000 per year as manager of the store. His family was Baptist but he has changed to Congregationalist to "escape religious dogma," and to obtain "more freedom of conscience." His wife is a Congregationalist and it is probably true that he changed religions at marriage. Neither he nor his wife attend church very often. He is a member of the Cosmopolitan Chamber of Commerce (a black civic association) and the Chatham-Avalon Park Community Council (the local community organization) and attends both. His wife is a block chairman for the latter organization. He contributes to the NAACP and has attended the rallies and marches of Dr. Martin Luther King in Chicago. He had no contact with whites where he grew up or in school but now has contact with whites every day at work and approximately once a month at his home, parties, and in voluntary organizations.

Is Present Contact Enough

No, I would like more in all areas. In a truly integrated society, there wouldn't be any limit to the contacts with whites. They could be neighbors, on the job everywhere. Then you would just be dealing with people, not any race, and there wouldn't be any marked differences.

Participation in Unorganized Protest

No, I've always believed in organized protest long before the civil rights groups. I was interested in group organization to procure better jobs for Negroes back in the early forties.

Negroes Passing

I have no particular objection to them. If it is a question of someone "passing," it's up to the individual to say what he is really. A person may "pass" for white or Negro.

Is African Ancestry an Advantage or a Disadvantage

Well, I don't really believe that Negroes came from Africa. I believe that they were brought from Africa. If they had come from Africa like other immigrants — the Irish from Ireland, the Italians from Italy, the English from England — then there would be no disadvantage. Other races of people who were not bonded were free to do as they pleased; they had certain rights. But the Negroes, having been brought here as slaves, were never accorded any of the dignities of man. In his position as a slave, he was regarded as a piece of property that had no human rights. He became so deeply imbedded in the social fabric of society that even when he became free the stigma was still attached to him.

Interracial Marriage

Interracial marriage is fine; I have no objections.

Opinion of Middle-Class Negro

This is a subject I really don't like to discuss. The middle-class Negro in the United States is really small in number, and it seems to me that he isn't comparable in many ways to the middle-class white American. I say this mainly because there is a difference in values between the two groups. It's difficult really to put into words. For example, community organization is highly efficient in a white middle-class community in the activities of their particular group, while the Negro middle-class has not yet learned how to effectively use the community organization as a tool. The whole scale of values just differs.

Opinion of Middle-Class Negro

The same as the lower-class white. He is largely a victim of social forces over which he has no control: lack of education, lower-paying jobs, poor housing.

CAN THE LOWER-CLASS NEGRO RISE FROM THE GHETTO

Certainly, because all other groups have; and given the same opportunities, the same access to employment, and the same access to education, there is no reason that I can see why Negroes can't function the same as other people in this society. If they call this the great melting pot, they will have to let them into the pot.

The respondent feels that it makes no difference whom he works alongside, but he would prefer to live in a neighborhood composed of half whites and half blacks because, "I would rather live in a mixed neighborhood because I happen to feel that it's only going to be by association that barriers are eventually going to be broken down among races." He would find no distaste in eating or dancing with whites, or in going to a party and finding it composed of all whites; and he would not mind a member of his family marrying a white person.

HOSTILITY TOWARD WHITES

I certainly feel angry sometimes. When I saw the picture of Medgar Evers' assassination and the brutality of the police in certain Southern states and the stubbornness of Superintendent Benjamin Willis in the school situation, I was very angry.

RELIEF OF HOSTILITY

It just sort of goes away, or you repress it as best you can, or I send another check to Martin Luther King.

This respondent noted that he feels less hostility toward whites now than he did when he was younger. He feels that he has been discriminated against a great deal, especially when he was younger, and had it not been for this discrimination he feels that he would have at least a Master's degree by now. He drinks very infrequently, but he reported three symptoms of stress — aches and pains and headaches one or two times, and nervousness and tenseness several times during the week previous to the interview.

Case No. 43 is a brown, forty-four-year-old attorney who is an executive in more than one firm. He was born and raised in a small Southern town by his mother. He stated that his father was a cowboy and died in Texas. He grew up with only one sister. His mother did not work but was a housewife, and he gives no indication of how the family was supported. He is married for the first time and his wife is a clerk for a governmental agency. He earned his B.A. and law degree in Chicago area universities. He earns in excess of $15,000 a year, and his wife earns an additional $5,000. He claims Baptist affiliation but attends the Baptist church only because "I happen to like the minister and I am able to help some people that I like. I hate to think of it as a preference. It would be all the same if it were Methodist or Catholic." Both he and his wife attend church practically every Sunday. He is an active member in five organizations: a Greek letter fraternity, the Chatham Community Council, two businessmen's organizations, and his church, of which he is on the board of trustees.

CIVIL RIGHTS PARTICIPATION

I sponsored, or I'd say the Chatham Park Manor Businessmen's Association sponsored, Martin Luther King in the park here last summer, and we contributed $1,000 to the recent freedom rally in the International Amphitheater. One of the reasons that I have not participated as fully as I would like to is that I am the manager of a banking association and I would not like my affiliations to be questioned at all. I've become a little more involved because I have become aware that I have not been participating as much as I should.

The respondent had contact with whites every day where he grew up, after school, daily while in the university and now meets with them every day at work. He comes in contact with whites in his home and at parties on an average of once a month and in voluntary organizations once a week.

IS PRESENT CONTACT ENOUGH

Yes, this is sufficient. Personally I'm just not fascinated by white people as such, and I can take them or leave them. I do not wish to extend myself for them unless we have something in common. My philosophy regarding my relationships with whites is somewhat tempered by my association with whites in college and all through life, so some of the glamor has worn off.

PARTICIPATION IN UNORGANIZED PROTEST

No, my sensitivity has never reduced myself to that level of neurotic behavior.

NEGROES PASSING

I have no dislike for a man who does what he feels. I would never consider it. If a man feels that he can better himself by this deception, then I think he should try it. One deception is no more of a deception than another; that is, a man who passes is like a woman who buys a wig or false eyelashes.

IS AFRICAN ANCESTRY AN ADVANTAGE OR A DISADVANTAGE

Neither. I don't feel that where a man comes from means anything in this day and age. What he is doing with himself now is important and what he can do. I could say that it's a disadvantage because African Negroes are treated better than American Negroes.

INTERRACIAL MARRIAGE

I have no particular feeling one way or the other. There should be no restrictions between man and woman.

OPINION OF MIDDLE-CLASS NEGRO

He doesn't have the time (to devote to the Civil Rights Movement). I think he's the most sensitive of the lot because he wonders where he is going. He is tolerant. He has the kind of association that is aloof. He doesn't want to get too close to the downtrodden Negro. The wealthy Negro tries to segregate himself from the one who tries to come up to his standard.

OPINION OF THE LOWER-CLASS NEGRO

He has little regard for law, even less for himself or anyone else. He is almost reduced to the level of an animal. He has to worry about his survival.

CAN THE LOWER-CLASS NEGRO RISE FROM THE GHETTO

It is remotely possible. First of all, in the ghetto he has a built-in anchor around his neck — welfare payments. Once he has tasted the nectar of the monthly check, he has no desire to find a job. ADC and the very things that have tried to help him are keeping him down.

The respondent feels that racial composition would make no difference either at work or in the neighborhood. He also would find none of the social distance items distasteful to him.

HOSTILITY TOWARD WHITES

Yes, sometimes. Whenever I read that certain things have been done to Negroes, such as the boy who was beaten to death in Cicero and the Palmer kid, I think I hate all of them.

RELIEF OF HOSTILITY

I don't do anything at all to relieve it. I don't think any overt action is necessary to release my feelings.

The respondent feels that he has been discriminated against a great deal in school and in jobs.

EFFECT OF DISCRIMINATION ON LIFE

They made me conscious of a great deal of my shortcomings. I think I was brainwashed into believing that if I could do something a little better than the white man, maybe he would accept me. I think perhaps I wanted to belong.

This respondent does not drink but owns two cars, one a Cadillac. He reported five symptoms of stress — cold sweats, loss of appetite, headaches, nervousness or tenseness, and rapid heartbeat one or two times — for the week preceding the interview.

Discussion

In both of these cases the respondent is over forty and has had some Southern experience. Both men have participated in the civil rights movement; Case No. 43 feels the constraints of his position in this area yet voices the desire to do more. One desires more contact with whites, which we would expect, but the other goes to great lengths to indicate that he is above all that now. Neither one has participated in unorganized protest. In terms of their heritage, the attorney makes the case for the achieving society and the clothing manager spells out the stigma of slavery. Both see marriage as a personal thing and do not object to inter-racial marriage. In great departure from the Benevolent's view, both of the Uncle Toms see nothing terribly wrong with blacks "passing." In their evaluation of middle-class blacks both respondents seem to hedge the issue. The store manager makes a comparison between the white and black middle class and concludes that there is a great difference in values between the two as is evidenced by the relatively inefficient community organization that middle-class blacks have in comparison to whites. In the other case, we hear the business man's ploy that "he doesn't have the time," and then a fairly accurate account of the inclination of the black middle class to segregate themselves from the lower class. If this is self-hate, it is of a muted variety. As for the lower-class black, both respondents see him as a poor victim of circumstances. Here, also, as in the case of the Benevolents, anti-white hostility is evoked not personally but through the mechanism of mass media, and the individual reacts either by sending a check to the civil rights cause or by repressing it. Both of these individuals indicate that their hostility towards whites is much less now than it was in the past, when they were younger. This is a critical point to remember, for there is a very real possibility that the placing of individuals along an interracial dimension is very dependent upon life cycle phenomena as well as upon situational experience. Finally, both of these cases reported several physiological symptoms of stress, although neither drinks to excess.

Race Men

Case No. 30 is a brown, forty-year-old accountant who operates his own tax service. He was born in a large Southern city, but was raised in Chicago by both parents along with one brother and four sisters. He is married for the first time and his wife works as a school teacher. He earns $11,000 as an accountant, and his wife earns an additional $8,000. He is a Black Muslim. Previous to this conviction he was a Lutheran, as is his wife. He belongs to the American Accounting association; and in the realm of civil rights, he is a member of the Urban League although he does not attend its meetings. He also teaches Negro history to children for the Frank London Brown Club. He reads *Muhammed Speaks* every week because "I enjoy this paper because you get the opposite version, whether it be true or not, than you get in other papers." He had contact with whites daily while growing up and in school, as he does now in the work situation. At home and in voluntary organizations he has none.

IS PRESENT CONTACT ENOUGH

Enough. It's just that I don't trust them. Too many of them try to be too friendly. I think most of them are frauds. Associating with Negroes makes them feel important because it makes them feel like they've done their good deed for the day.

The respondent has not participated in unorganized protest.

Negroes Passing

I think it is an individual thing and depends upon a person's values. There is no question that he can do better economically; it just depends on what he values most.

Is African Ancestry an Advantage or a Disadvantage

I don't think it is either one. I don't see what difference it makes. Black people are viewed the same in this country no matter where they come from.

Interracial Marriage

If people of different races or religions want to get married, they should be strong enough to face the problems they impose on themselves.

Opinion of Middle-Class Negro

The most spineless person in the United States. He is too comfortable economically. It is only when he loses his comforts that he is going to start participating in civil rights.

Opinion of Lower-Class Negro

Generally, they are unaware. They don't know who to vote for other than who the precinct captain tells him when he presents him with a gift. Generally, they are no different from impoverished groups anywhere. These people are too involved with just living to involve themselves in community projects or anything above the daily strain of existing till the next day.

Can the Lower-Class Negro Rise from the Ghetto

It is doubtful because their particular conditions perpetuate themselves through the action or non-action of governmental units and others.

Racial Mixture on the Job

I have worked alongside and with both. The friction that develops is as often between black and black, or white and white, as between black and white. It appears that on jobs it has more to do with personalities than with race, since racial prejudice is masked quite well on jobs.

Racial Mixture in Neighborhood

When it comes to neighbors, socializing, anything that has to do with off-the-job contacts, I just prefer to be around my own.

This respondent is one of the few who spells out a specific notion of the differences between the races:

One big difference between groups is attitudes. Negroes have a greater disregard for other people's rights than other groups of people. Primarily, they have a greater disregard for the rights of other Negroes. This is the result of over 300 years of conditioning. They've been taught that Negroes have no rights.

This respondent claims he would not find it distasteful to eat and dance with, or have someone in his family marry, a white person, although he would have earlier in life. As in the case of an earlier example, this respondent would find it extremely distasteful to go to a party and find it consisted of all whites.

Hostility Toward Whites

Yes, generally. I feel that behind each one of those smiling faces, who proclaim that their best friend is a Negro, lies most of our problem.

This respondent feels that he has not suffered much discrimination other than exclusion from certain types of positions.

Although most of the respondents held negative attitudes toward Mayor Daley and Congressman Dawson, the Race Men generally were the most critical. This respondent's verbalizations are typical of this intense attitude.

Opinion of Mayor Daley

Worst thing that could have been foisted upon the population of Chicago, especially the black population. "King" Richard and his six "house niggers" have completely shown their disrespect for the black population in futherance of their own political aims.

Opinion of Congressman Dawson

Dawson is just "Uncle Dawson," and this attitude has been hardened somewhat by a speech made by him some years ago in connection with Federal aid to schools in which he suggested that even though Negro chlidren were not receiving proper education, Negroes should do nothing that would interfere with the dear little children.

This respondent reported that he drinks only occasionally and claimed only one symptom of distress — skin rashes.

Case No. 30 is a dark brown, twenty-six-year-old registered pharmacist and manager of a chain drugstore. He was born in Mississippi but was raised in Chicago by both parents. He was an only child. He is married and has one pre-school age daughter; his wife works as a clerk. He received all of his public school and college education in Chicago. He claims an income of $15,000 per year and his wife earns an additional $3,000. He has no religious preference although his wife is a Baptist. He belongs to no voluntary organizations, nor does his wife. He contributes money to the NAACP. He now has contact with whites once a week or more in his home, at work, and at parties. This same pattern was experienced while he was growing up.

Is Present Contact Enough

Enough. Some of my experiences with whites have left a bad taste in my mouth, and the less contact with them, the better off I'll be.

This respondent has never participated in unorganized protest.

Negroes Passing

They confirm every belief about them that white people have ever had because they are trying to get away from what they are. I feel sorry for them because they have to deny their own existence in order to get what they want.

Is African Ancestry an Advantage or a Disadvantage

Neither one. I don't think it matters.

Interracial Marriage

I feel sorry for them. They are ostracised by the white community and the Negro community. In fact, I should say that I admire them because they are living in a world all by themselves and this takes some kind of special strength.

OPINION OF MIDDLE-CLASS NEGRO

Some of them tend to forget that they are Negroes. They are like a separate breed. Some of them tend to divorce themselves from the rest of the Negro group. They attribute their success to themselves and think they need no one else.

OPINION OF LOWER-CLASS NEGRO

It is a web of not enough education, prejudice, and lack of desire in which they are trapped like caged animals. They can't get enough to get ahead. It kills their initiative and it is passed on to their children.

CAN THE LOWER-CLASS NEGRO RISE FROM THE GHETTO

They can, providing that you educate them. Education is the key to the whole thing. You have to give them a goal to work for. I feel that no matter what your color, you don't want to live in dirt. The rumor that they don't want to live any better is just that. It is spread around to ease a lot of troubled consciences.

This respondent would rather work in a mixed situation:

It kind of inspires both to do just a little bit better because he (a white worker) isn't going to let you outdo him and you are certainly not going to let him outdo you. When we work together (Negro with Negro) we are inclined to have feuds and cliques.

This respondent has no preference for a racial mixture in his neighborhood but would find all of the social distance items distasteful to him.

HOSTILITY TOWARD WHITES

Yes, when I'm deprived of something merely because I'm a Negro.

The respondent did not elaborate further on this statement and mentioned no mechanisms for relief of hostility. In response to the question asking for specific instances of discrimination, he mentioned a rather minor threater incident and a restaurant incident and said that they affected him quite a bit. Both of these happened on the north side of Chicago. He remarked about the effect of these instances, "It gave me the drive to get a profession. Instead of killing my drive, it inspired me to go on to be as much or more than the ones who snubbed me and segregated themselves from me."

The respondent drinks every day and was high during the previous week. He reported four symptoms of stress — cold sweats, a common cold, nervousness or tenseness, and an upset stomach — in the previous week also.

In addition to the two cited cases of the Race Men type, we would like to add a short description of an emergent Race Man. This case is interesting, for it clearly shows the attitude change of an individual. The respondent is a fair (unusual for this type), thirty-nine-year-old professional psychologist. He comes from a well-to-do family in which his father was a minister and his mother a teacher. Both parents held college degrees. He was born and raised in Northern cities and holds a Ph.D. from a Chicago university. He has contact with whites once or more a week in his home, at parties, and in voluntary organizations. In response to this contact, he states:

> It is enough for me, maybe too much. I think that one of the problems is the slowness and resistance to the civil rights movement. I feel fed up with whites in general. I feel a hostility toward them that I haven't felt before.

He is very active in civil rights and states that he is attending more and more meetings because "I, like many others, have gotten caught up in this thing because we who are older did not participate as much as before. Now we have children and we feel the need more now than before." This disposition, in part, started with individual protest when the respondent was younger. "I can recall back in Michigan I used to go around knocking the heads off the blackamoor figures that whites used to have on their lawns." In response to the question on hostility toward whites, the respondent explicitly states again his emergent feelings, "Yes, I'm getting that way (hostile). I didn't before age thirty, but I am gaining this kind of hostility fast. The driving force is their apathy toward the civil rights movement. I think there are too many who either feel apathetic or are actually hostile toward the Negro. I talk about this to release a lot of my tensions. I talk to my wife or to some of my white friends whom I can talk to."

Discussion

For this type we have a representative of all three age categories and the three shades of skin coloring. The amount of interracial contact varies, but one common characteristic that stands out — other than a negative attitude toward whites — is that of Northern background.[2] Another common attitude is that all three respondents sympathize with the lower-class black and attribute his plight to the control of the white man. The element of African nationalism, although somewhat present from the fact that one individual is a Black Muslim, is not very strong as none feels any great affinity with African heritage. All are critical of the middle-class black for not doing more to advance the race, and all generally prefer to be among members of their own race. None desire any more contact with whites than they now have. None of these individuals expressed the feeling that they had been greatly discriminated against, and in the accounts that they reported, indeed, none of them had seriously suffered. Nevertheless, they all were deeply affected by these instances of discrimination they had perceived.

The patterns that these individuals follow is interesting in that age seems to operate in both directions on attitudes toward whites. The young pharmacist is anti-white and his feeling seems to stem from two meager instances of discrimination which prompted him to strive for a profession. The older accountant has changed to Muslim belief later in life and yet reports that he is more accepting of whites now than he was when he was younger. Finally, in the case of the psychologist it appears that, although he performed some anti-white acts as a youth, he is rapidly approaching a decidedly anti-white position because of his increasing involvement in civil rights and his perception of the apathy of the white citizenry about this movement. He also mentions that concern for his children brought pressure upon him to act in this manner. Concern for children may be a significant factor in changing interracial attitudes. This factor is reinforced by the author's discovery of a parallel case. Early in

---

[2]The reason for this is quite clear. Up to the birth of the civil rights movement in the 1960's, the pattern of sensitivity to discrimination on the part of blacks seemed to follow the pervasiveness of the color bar and the severity of negative sanctions imposed when race etiquette was breached. Therefore by region, Southern blacks were more sensitive to patterns of discrimination than Northern blacks with those black persons living in the border states falling in between. (See Johnson 1943; Banks 1950, pp. 529-34). Then during the 1960s the pattern of sensitivity changed and began to follow the discrepancy between the expected behavior of whites and their actual response to black demands. So, when Southern blacks expected Southern whites to react to the civil rights movement in an extremely negative manner and they did, it caused no great revelation. But when Northern blacks expected a positive response on civil rights from Northern whites and the whites comment was either apathetic or betrayed their bigotry and racism this produced anti-white hostility in Northern black persons far in excess of that found among Southern blacks. It is not surprising then that it was the North and the West that produced Malcolm X, Eldridge Cleaver, and Stokely Carmichael.

this study the author interviewed several families himself for up to six hours in an undirected manner in order to gain familiarity with the problems involved. One case in these early interviews showed the effect that children can have on interracial attitudes which is strikingly similar to that of the psychologist. The individual was a high-ranking insurance executive who also owned an apartment building in fashionable Hyde Park. The author was surprised to find out that the individual had participated in the march on Selma. Probing of this area revealed that the individual himself had no proclivities toward civil rights action as he was doing very well as matters stood. However, he had a daughter in school at the time who came home one day and announced that she had to go to Selma because she felt that she could not live with herself if she did not go. Her motivation was so strong that the pleas of her parents could not deter her. So the father accompanied her for no personal reasons other than to see to her safety. He came back a changed man who now can no longer ignore the movement. The point to be made here is the effect of children on the attitudes of the parents. Both of these cases show increased involvement in the civil rights movement and increasing hostility toward whites due to consideration of their children's future.

In summary, a very complex pattern emerges for this type. A young black man feels hostility toward whites because of some minor incidences of discrimination. An older black man simultaneously follows an anti-white line by becoming a Muslim and becomes more pro-white by accepting behavior of and contact with whites that he would not have accepted in the past. Finally, the impact of the civil rights movement can clearly be seen in the two cases of the psychologist and the executive who are becoming more and more anti-white because of their increased involvement.

World Haters

Case No. 2 is a brown, forty-nine-year-old internal revenue supervisor. He was born in a large Southern city, but was raised in Chicago by both parents. He was a member of a fairly large family consisting of four sisters and two brothers. His father had a college degree but worked as a janitor. He is married for the second time, having divorced his first wife. They have one child in public school and his wife does not work. He received all his public school and college education in Chicago and has a year of graduate work. He claims an income of only $12,000 per year; but in response to the question asking if he had an additional source of income, he said that he would not tell either the source or the amount, so it is probable that he earns much more. He reports that he is a Catholic but attends church only "when forced" by his wife who attends every Sunday. He changed religion from Methodist to Catholic, but he gave no reason for the change. The only organization that he belongs to is a golf club which he attends very regularly. He does not participate in civil rights in any way. He has contact with whites every day at work and had contact with them every day while growing up and in school. He attends interracial parties once a week and has whites in his home on an average of once per month.

Is Present Contact Enough

I'm happy. It is enough for me; in fact, it is too much for me. I'm not concerned. If I wanted more, I could have more. I'm happy.

In response to the question asking whether or not he had ever participated in unorganized protest, he replied, "No, I like white folks, they've been nice to me." The interviewer noted that he said this in a very facetious manner.

Negroes Passing

If he can benefit himself by "passing", fine.

Is African Ancestry an Advantage or a Disadvantage

It would not make any difference where Negroes came from. The fact of skin coloration is the only problem.

Interracial Marriage

No sweat, no problem. Nothing to me. It is compatibility that counts.

Opinion of Middle-Class Negro

More often than not, he is a brown-noser or user of other people in the U.S.A. The white-collar Negro in a white organization nosed his way in. In Negro organizations he has taken advantage of some Negroes.

Opinion of Lower-Class Negro

More often than not, he is a victim of circumstance. It is a congenital problem and an environmental problem.

CAN THE LOWER-CLASS NEGRO RISE FROM THE GHETTO

No.

When asked what racial composition he would prefer to work with, the respondent replied that it made no difference. "I'm not prejudiced. I'm a class-conscious Negro. I dő not like poor anything." A racially mixed neighborhood would not affect him at all, and he felt no distaste about any of the social distance items.

HOSTILITY TOWARD WHITES

Yes, I don't like stupid whites in the same position I'm in. I indicate or point out their stupidity. At times, I hate stupid whites. If they are above me, they are unqualified practitioners.

RELIEF OF HOSTILITY

I get me a drink after work when I have fits of anger. At work I write memorandums using pedantic language.

The respondent claims that he feels less hostility toward whites than he did at age thirty. He feels he has suffered little from racial discrimination and most of that was felt during high school. He is quite an outdoorsman: he owns a boat, swims, and goes fishing quite frequently in addition to playing golf. He shoots pool regularly and plays cards and bowls every week. He drinks at home every day and in taverns when he has had a frustrating day, but he gave no indication of overindulgence. He mentioned that he suffered general aches and pains, nervousness, and tenseness several times during the week previous to the interview.

Case No. 7 is a brown, forty-seven-year-old family support counselor. He was born and raised in the South by both parents and came to Chicago when he was thirty-three years old. He grew up with six brothers and sisters. His father was a farmer and his mother a housewife; neither had any formal education beyond the sixth grade. He has one son of his own in a public grade school. He is married to his first wife who works as a public school teacher. His wife's father was a Methodist minister and her mother a schoolteacher. He attended all-Negro schools in the South and holds a B.A. degree from a Southern all-Negro college. He was raised a Baptist but switched to Methodism upon marriage. Both are very strong Methodists and attend church every Sunday. The only organization that he belongs to is a Methodist men's organization of which he is president. He has no contact at all with whites. He gives money and has marched for two of the more militant civil rights organizations, SNCC and CORE.

Is Present Contact Enough

This is enough. I'm not in love with white people and don't especially enjoy being around them.

Participation in Unorganized Protest

No, because I knew they would just put the signs (Colored Only or White Only) right back. I also knew that wasn't the kind of action our people needed.

Negroes Passing

No feeling whatsoever. It's their business as to what they choose to be.

Is African Ancestry an Advantage or a Disadvantage

A disadvantage, because the Negro was thrown into a different culture from what we had known and was expected to completely throw away his culture and absorb the white man's way of life.

Interracial Marriage

To each his own. Everyone has the right to choose his own "misery" from whatever race he wants.

Opinion of Middle-Class Negro

It's the same as my opinion of the white-collar white man. They are struggling to make a place for themselves in this world.

Opinion of Lower-Class Negro

I sympathize with him because of his lack of motivation and lack of opportunity. I feel he can be helped with proper training and motivation.

Can the Lower-Class Negro Rise from the Ghetto

They certainly can rise from the ghettos just as the Irish, the Jew, and the Italian has done.

The racial mixture of his place of work or residence makes no difference to him, for he states, "I feel that I am qualified to work with any human being, white or Negro," and as for neighborhood, "It would make no difference so long as they don't endanger my life or destroy my property." He also would feel no distaste about any of the social distance items.

HOSTILITY TOWARD WHITES

Yes, I feel hostility to all humans at times, not necessarily whites. I do think I feel hostile quicker towards whites.

RELIEF OF HOSTILITY

It depends on the situation. I usually express my opinions in no uncertain terms.

He feels that he has suffered a great deal of discrimination in school, on the job, and in housing, especially when he was in his early twenties. It affected him very much, as he states:

It made me hostile to a certain degree. Also it has made me feel I have to work twice as hard as the white man in order to succeed or be on the same level with him.

The respondent plays cards and golfs every week and drinks every day, usually at home. During the week preceding the interview he complained of a cold and headaches.

Discussion

These two cases are quite different in terms of background. One was raised and educated in the South; the other, in the North. Although both are older men, they differ in their amount of interracial contact and in their participation in civil rights. Neither has a positive word to say about whites, and the revenue supervisor detests their stupidity. Neither takes a stand on interracial marriage. Both feel that the lower-class black is a victim of circumstance, and they differ greatly in their opinion of the middle-class black man. One feels that he is a user of his own race and a pawn of the white man, and the other thinks that he is just trying to make a place in this world.

One significant common element between the two is that they utilize either verbal or written expression in response to their feelings of anti-white hostility, a response which is rare over the sample as a whole.

Most of the other respondents would not give a mechanism of relief. Neither places any emphasis on racial mixture either at work or at residence, but rather they place their evaluations on a personal common value and individual basis, which is indicative of their lack of group affiliation or identification. Another indication of this is their activity in leisure time pursuits. Neither does much in an organizational setting; they act alone in personal pursuits. Finally, both indicated symptoms of stress, and in addition, the "class-conscious" one stated that he drank every day.

Conclusions

The basic questions to be answered from this analysis are: From the construction of this typology what further clarification of knowledge do we have concerning the attitudinal and behavioral patterns of the black middle class, and how is this typology related to those previously constructed? The first and most obvious conclusion we can draw is that there is a great deal of mixing and blending of reactions to minority group status, and these reactions are not necessarily dependent upon the amount of discrimination or oppression perpetrated on the individual. For each of our types, we can find evidence of intropunitive and extropunitive reaction. For each, we can perceive movement toward and against the oppressor and very little tendency to move away from him.

With our typology we can also identify patterns that were previously hidden or obscured from observation. A major pattern is that of attitude change over time. With the indications that we have, in the form of differing ages for differing types, and using retrospective analysis, we would assert that interracial stance is closely tied to life cycle. Younger members tend to be more positively disposed toward both races, although less so toward the white. Then as the life process unfolds, epecially if geographical movement takes the individual to the Southern states, and competition in the occupational sphere occurs, the individual begins to experience either the failings of members of his own race to advance the cause or the bigotry and apathy of the white man toward the plight of the mass of black people. He then gradually changes his heretofore accepting ways and begins to feel a hostility toward one race or the other, and in some cases, both.

There is also a counter trend appearing in the case studies. This is manifested in that even with an increase in hostility and negative feelings toward the white man, there appears a mellowing and an acceptance of interracial marriage and interracial contact to which the individual was previously opposed. We would also argue that the civil rights movement has been instrumental in instigating militance and forcing those who were divorced from the realities of black subordination to become aware of the situation, change their attitude, and try to do something about it. It is true that the safest route — donating money and not jeopardizing one's own safe position, as exemplified by the case of the attorney who had to protect his banking association — is the one most often taken, but a substantial proportion of the black middle class does more.

It is clear that inroads have been made into the previously defined situation where the middle-class black insulated himself into an all middle-class life space and gave no consideration at all to racial advancement.

In addition to the change in attitudes along the age dimension, we also note the predicted difference by color or skin shade. Those who are most identifiable as black by their pigmentation are those most likely to identify with their race and hold the highest feelings of militance, namely, the Race Man. The lightest type blacks (the World Haters), instead of identifying with whites, hold negative dispositions toward both races and are very cosmopolitan in their outlook. They do not see, or at least try not to see, the world in color or race terms, but rather they think in terms of personality, achievement orientation, and common middle-class value standards. The element of "class-consciousness" is strongest within this type.

These four groups differ in social status as measured by income, occupation, and education, as well as in behavioral areas, the most notable of which is their expressive mechanisms of tension release. Here we find that those who hold the most stressful interracial positions evidence the greatest amount of physiological symptoms of stress as well as higher incidence of alcohol consumption.

Thus, we would argue that these analytic types do have distinguishing characteristics and that knowledge of them is very useful in understanding the differentiation among middle-class blacks. These differing types and their correlates provide a basis for the construction of a model of race relations within the black middle class. We will present this model in the concluding chapter.

6

The Life History

of

Robert Black

This chapter will be devoted to a description of the life history of Robert Black.[1] We present this account for it illustrates the generic development of a black middle-class man by revealing the factors that have molded the life of this individual within his cultural setting. By tracing the sequences of events that influenced this man's life we are in a much better position to understand how American society and culture and our institutions affect the middle-class black American.

The reader should pay close attention to the institutions and particular individuals that affected this man's life. But more important, the reader should be aware of the complicated and interactive factors that make up Robert Black's racial stance. The development of his inter- and intraracial position and how this in turn influences his thoughts and actions is the dynamic process which this life history details more fully than any of the preceding analysis. At the end of the chapter we will relate this life history to our analytic typology.

I was born in 1932, in a small town in Tennessee. My father was a tenant farmer for a white man who owned several farms in the surrounding area. He did things as a tenant farmer such as plowing the

---

[1] We present the case of Robert Black as a member of a socio-racial group — the black middle class. He does not represent the group as a whole and he is neither typical nor atypical. His life history is not evidence to validate a hypothesis but rather it is presented to provide the richness of detail to enhance understanding. For the strengths as well as the weaknesses of the life history method, see: Allport 1942; Blumer 1939; Bain 1929; Dollard 1935; and Young 1966.

fields, planting grain, and harvesting. We lived in a very small two-bedroom shack back from the road. My uncle also lived there with his wife and a couple of kids and maybe two or three other tenant farmers.

One of my aunts worked in the landowner's home as a cook and a maid. My mother worked in a canning factory in the town. I don't know how far out in the country we lived at that point but I suppose maybe six or ten miles from town. My dad had the use of a car; it was a roadster with a rumble seat.

I was the only child born to the marriage of my mother and father. My father had been married previously and maybe had been married twice previously; but I knew that I had a half sister and brother.

In Tennessee, at this point in time, land was available and farms were spread out. There just weren't too many neighbors. The fellow my dad worked for had these three or four shacks behind the plantation. I don't know whether it was a plantation or not. Up the main road leading to this place were two other houses that black people lived in. Down the road were some friends of the family and they had a young kid my age and a daughter maybe a couple of years older than I was. My half brother lived somewhere in the town and we used to visit with each other. He would come over and we would spend the night with each other. I'm talking now about the period of time from when I was born until the time I was four years old.

My mom's dad, I am told, delivered me while chopping cotton and all these other kinds of things. You put the bag of cotton down and you have the baby and you keep on picking the cotton. My mother is from a family of fifteen kids. Whether my grandfather was my grandmother's first, second, or third husband, I really don't know. Or whether any of the fellows she had children with were her actual husbands, I don't know. That grandmother is still alive, although I've never broached her dignity to ask her as to whether all her kids were legitimate or illegitimate. I think I've been interested in that thing but that's not a thing you ask your grandmother. I'll say some more about that later.

I was illegitimate. My parents were not married when I was born, and I don't know whether my dad was married to his first wife at the time, or just didn't marry my mother at that point. I only discovered this later when I decided to enlist in the service when I finished high school. I was legally illegitimate; their relationship was legally illegitimate, but I feel that I was a legitimate child.

My great-grandfather had, some years earlier, with his wife moved to Dixon[2] (a middle-sized industrial city in the Midwest). He was an

---

[2]Dixon is not the true name of the city.

employee of the Wabash Railroad. I don't know what he did but I suppose he was a porter or something of this sort. I really hadn't thought about it that much, but I guess he was nearing retirement slightly before or about the time of the depression. He had a home in Dixon and had bought an additional lot on the east side of Dixon which is pretty much of a "ghetto" today. There was a scattering of white families in the area, but the majority were blacks. He had brought his son, my mother's dad, to Dixon some years before because job opportunities were better. Brawn was the thing you needed, not brains. Dixon was, as it is today, a very industrialized city. There were more job opportunities for unskilled blacks in Dixon than there might have been in the South which was at this point a basically agricultural economy.

My dad was still working for this white person who owned many farms when I left Tennessee. I was four or four and a half when I moved to Dixon. My great-grandfather took me to his son's house. This was in early or late spring of 1936 or 1937.

I remember that there was no such thing as a kindergarten at that time in Dixon. There was a pre-school, but it was kind of a day-care center, operated out of the interest of a particular woman who got some community support to get some materials, in a vacant building that was diagonally across the street from my grandparents' residence. Directly across the street from my grandparents lived my grandfather's sister, her husband and I guess her son and perhaps his wife. I remember being disciplined by my aunt, my great aunt, as much as by my grandparents. They enrolled me in the day-care school that September.

My parents came to Dixon in October or November of that year. It's kind of interesting because my mother came first and my dad followed her maybe two weeks or two months later. I didn't know who she was at first and I'd just been away from her since March. I remember I started crying and I was very glad to see her.

So my dad joined us later and we lived with my grandfather maybe a year until I entered first grade. My dad got a job at one of the filling stations in Dixon. One of the guys who lived next door to my grandparents has become my lifelong friend. We grew up together, starting out with tricycles. One of the first things my grandparents bought me was a tricycle. We would ride it all the way across the street to the day-care center.

I started first grade at Duncan School, which was about 65 percent black, in Dixon. I was at Duncan School for the second semester and when promotion time came I was told by the teacher: "You are not promoted. We want to keep you back because you are such a good blackboard eraser and cleaner of erasers. We want to keep you back and do this." I guess this was her way of telling me that I hadn't really "cut the mustard" with the rest of the class. I didn't think too much about it. I was proud that I was recognized as a good eraser cleaner, but a little bit pained by the fact that I wasn't able to go on with my friends at that point. Well, I got over that in a couple of months and they did let me clean the erasers. They had a little machine that they run them across, and it would snatch the chalk out of them.

That same year my parents moved into a section of a house. It might have been two bedrooms, one for me and one for my parents. Downstairs was a living room and a kitchen with an eating area. So we moved over to the south end of Dixon and I think that you need to understand Dixon. Residentially, it has been integrated for a number of years. Now to say it has been integrated doesn't mean that black people have lived all over the city, but they have lived in the major areas of the town except exclusive residential areas which have been economically exclusive since 1937. There were pockets of blacks. There were several grade schools, only four or five junior high schools, and only one senior high school when I was growing up. So you know your education was always an integrated thing. Duncan School, which was on the east side of town, was probably the only school that had the majority of black kids going to it. The other schools were all predominately white. So I'm saying that I've never been in an all-black school, that I can remember. In fact, I've never had a black teacher. The first black teacher came to Dixon when I was out of the service.

When I was eight or nine, there was a drawing at a neighborhood grocery store and the first prize was a bicycle and I won it, at least my parents did from buying groceries. You put the little number of the stub in the box and I won this silly thing. I used to traverse the major concentration of black neighborhoods because I had an aunt out in one end of town, and a grandmother in another end, and I lived in the other end of town. I'd ride my bike and spend a couple of nights or overnight, like Friday night, with my aunt out in the west end of town; that's where Ann (future wife) lived, and we grew up together, went to Sunday School together. Her dad was superintendent of Sunday School. Other weekends I would go to the east end of town and stay with my grandmother and grandfather, and I would have my recreation with my friends out there. I was going to a black section in each instance, because this was a circumscribed area of eight to ten blocks on the west end that the majority of blacks lived in.

From the second grade to the sixth I went to Washington Grade School in Dixon. I don't know what the racial balance of Washington

Grade School was but I suppose it was probably 80 percent white and 20 percent black. At that point I can only remember in my classes maybe two, three, or four black kids. At the grade school level I had the same access to basketball and other sports as most of the other kids did. Sports weren't discriminatory you know; there just wasn't a big thing about sports.

The break-off point came maybe when you were in the ninth grade. You were big enough to look like something and smart enough to recognize something that looked good to you, and you made moves at it that parents were fearful of. From maybe third grade to the sixth or seventh grade you would get invited to your teammates' birthday parties and occasionally other parties through the year. Then all of a sudden when you got just about to the eighth or ninth grade you stopped getting invited to birthday parties at your white friends' houses. That was kind of confusing you know. Here's a guy you shoot marbles with after school; you go to his house, he's at yours and maybe he has a sister and many of them did, and pretty soon you weren't invited anymore. You ask yourself why, and then things sort of come to you. But, your parents kind of tell you what's happening too. Because at that particular point in time there was not open occupancy as such. Nor were there public accommodation laws at this point either. The beach was segregated at that time. There was a fence that ran down the quarter of the very slimy beach which was fed by a man-made lake. There was a fence that separated you from the white swimmers. They gave you maybe sixty feet of sand and maybe they had 240 feet. You couldn't go into the public bath house and change clothes but you could swim in that water, however, you were downstream.

Well, anyhow we accepted this and we didn't think too much about it except to think it was unfair. Ann's dad was one of the earlier people to take a stand against the bigotry at the beach. Hell, he was a social protestor in his own time. He was a self-educated man. I know he didn't finish high school and he had no college degree. He was well read and a very religious man; but a very "with it" kind of guy. He could relate to young people. I think I was influenced by him quite a bit in terms of commitment to what was right and what was wrong and doing something about what was wrong.

In the south end of town there was a Baptist church and a Methodist church for blacks. The Baptist church was where her father was superintendent of Sunday School and where I started going when I was seven or eight. That's where I met her. We were in the seven-year-old Sunday School class. Also at that time, Dixon had four or five public parks and recreation programs connected with those parks in different

parts of town. I belonged to the south side recreation park; she belonged
to what was called Lincoln Park in the west end. We had a softball
team and we would go out and play against her softball team. So we
had contacts recreationally and also attending a common church. But,
she went to school in a totally different part of town than I did. In fact,
those of us on the south end of town and on the east end of town would
kind of look upon her end of town as kind of "uppity" because this
is where the majority of the rich whites lived at that time. She went to
school with the majority of rich white kids. We always thought that the
west end girls were kind of the cream of the crop.

My mother was about eighteen when she had me. She came from
the South. She was the fifth oldest child of fifteen and didn't complete
her education because she had to stay home and help her mom take care
of the other kids. I think the relationship with my father was an escape
from that for her, and they did later marry. But I've not gotten hung
up on my illegitimate or my illegal birth. Ann and I have been married
nineteen years and I think I've only told her that in the last nine years.
Ann is from a very large family too. Let me see, she still has six brothers
living and two sisters living. Her mother died during childbirth with her
youngest brother. She's never really known her mother, because her
father raised the family pretty much by himself. She was born and raised
in Dixon.

I never got hung up on these things until you start noticing certain
things. But, just like I said, her father exerted a certain kind of influence
on me. The minister in the church had a totally negative influence on
me because he scared the hell out of me. He came out of the South
and had a Southern orientation as far as religion is concerned. You're
going to hell if you play cards, if you dance, if you wear lipstick, if you
do all the things for which you may receive some credit for being a
human and expressing yourself as being a human being; you're going
to hell. Hell was described as some big cat, some Faustian dude with
the ears and the pitchfork turning you over for ever and ever. This was
the fantasy and the cat was very literate in his descriptions about what
hell was like. Catholics can describe purgatory in terms of how they
have been educated to believe and think of purgatory as a step between
here and something else. But the black Baptist minister was very harsh,
very explicit, and very graphic in his description of what hell was like
and the pain that one must pay for his sins committed here on earth.
I suppose it acted as a control for some people, temporarily to assist
them in resisting temptation. This was the big hell-fire and brimstone

thing. But anyway that scared the hell out of me. Later, you know, later adolescence, there was a point in time where you were made to stay for church. I don't know whether you dig that or not, but we kind of liked to go to Sunday School; that was from 9:30 to 10:30 or 11 o'clock and church started from 11 to 1 o'clock or whenever this cat decided to stop blowing.

As long as my mother had control, disciplinary control at least, you had to stay for church. You went to Sunday School, but you also had to stay and listen to all this gaff from this cat. Ann had to stay for church. She really had to stay because her dad was the superintendent of Sunday School. My mom was an usher so I had to stay for church too. You would have to sit there and listen to all this business and you know you go away from there scared. But then when I was twelve, I didn't join the church voluntarily. I expressed no interest in it and my mother stopped making me stay to church. I went to Sunday School out of my own desire to go which pleased her, but yet I didn't have to deal with this cat, who was more of a devil than I could conjure up in retrospect. So you start going and doing your own thing after church on Sunday. Ann and I would meet if she could get away from it. It was a groupy kind of thing during early adolescence. It was fun and it was nice.

I think I'm a very religious type of person but I don't believe that you have to attend an edifice to express this. I think it's a thing you do from Monday at 7 o'clock to the next Monday at 6:59. I don't go to church unless the kids are involved in something. I don't even go to church when Ann asks me, really. I go to church on Mother's Day and take my mother and grandmother but I usually avoid going to Dixon on Mother's Day to hang away from that thing. My church is the golf course pretty much in the summer on Sunday mornings. In the winter I use Sunday mornings to sleep late or go to the bowling alley and I don't consider myself irreligious. I think I have some very strong beliefs about human nature and people and how they are to be treated. I go through all these things but I just can't dig the antiquated notion that you still find in these predominantly black churches and black ministry that God is a very punitive kind of thing. Ann and the kids attend the Unitarian church on occasion. Ann still likes to go to the Baptist church. But it's a much more enlightened ministry now, please understand this. The point is that even though the minister is more enlightened, some of the parishioners or congregation are just as old school as they ever were and I don't feel that I ought to waste my time being bothered with that mentality about life and living. Listen to them say "Amen" to something that is extraneous or irrelevant as far as I am concerned is a waste of time. If that is what they dig, they can have it. It is not my bag. So, I just don't fool with it although I am a good friend of both ministers at the Baptist and Unitarian church.

Going back to this business of the ninth grade, as I said this is the cut-off point. I think you have to look at all these other things in context of that particular kind of growing up. School is the main continuation thread and the other things that impinge upon this are tangential to it. School was fine even though the teacher couldn't teach white history or black history. She taught history as she saw it, or as she was told to teach it and you heard the same history that the white kids heard, depending upon your level of interest, motivation, smarts, or what-have-you. You dug it; you picked it up, and you regurgitated it, and you moved on through the grade levels.

At this point in time, discrimination was a problematic thing. There was no open occupancy, no public accommodation laws, etc. You knew where you were welcomed, and if you didn't and you went in there naively, you were soon to be given an understanding of it. We could go into stores and my mother could try clothes on me and things of this sort to see if they fit without having to buy them forever. But there were certain places where you knew you could go and you couldn't go. You sat in the balcony in the theater, you didn't sit on the first floor.

But the dramatic shift in black-white relationships was in the ninth grade. I started to play basketball and football. I made the freshman varsity in basketball and football. You played freshman games and you could travel with the varsity teams. I remember going to other towns in the Midwest to play ball. As soon as a black cat got the ball the song was "Get that Nigger." They had gotten it down to a chant you know. It was a song and they sang it. It wasn't just an idle statement by one bigoted fan, it was a group thing, "Get him, get that Nigger." I remember that and I remember that it only made me run that much harder and I think that it went the same way for some of the other black cats on the team. The basketball coach was a guy who recognized talent, not color. And as long as I can remember he had some black players on his basketball teams.

Football was the same way, probably only worse because football was a more attacking game. It was kind of like boxing. It was the black cat against the white cat; this kind of thing probably not as sharply defined as you have on a one-to-one situation. But the venom was much more pronounced by the fans, and again it only made you strive that much harder to do your thing. It really got you into it.

When you look back on it, it is kind of funny because professionally I have worked all the towns that I used to know. There have been rare occasions when I have encountered any racial animosity. Nothing from adults — usually from children hanging out of the window of a station wagon. I recall several weeks ago when I was going to a meeting in one small town. I parked my car and had gotten out. It was in early evening, kind of dusk, and I had gone around to the trunk of the car to put my topcoat in it and get my briefcase. There was a little girl in a car, she couldn't have been over four or five. They were in a line of traffic and she said, "Hi Nigger!" I did not say anything, I just kept getting into my car and thinking to myself "poor kid." She said, "Nigger Hi," and I didn't say anything. Their car was stopped in a line of traffic waiting for the light to change, and she said, "Mommy that nigger won't say hi to me." Her mother had kind of slipped down into the seat. I felt she was thinking "Is he going to throw the fire-bomb or what is he going to do?"

My dad got killed on a motorcycle when I was ten, in 1942. At the time he died, my mother and he had separated and divorced and my mother had remarried. He had worked on WPA, and at the filling station. He had a lot of menial jobs because he didn't have a skill as such but I think he was a talented kind of guy in terms of mechanical things to work on cars and just about do anything. You didn't go down to a big car garage and get a job as an auto mechanic in those days. You worked at filling stations, washing cars and doing those sort of things. That is what he did. He worked and saved enough money to buy himself a Harley-Davidson or Indian, I forget, but I remember enjoying riding on it and that's how he was killed.

My stepfather still lives and he is a person that I have known as my dad for the last twenty-eight years; a wonderful kind of guy. He never laid a hand on me and has been in my corner all the way. He saved me from more trouble with my mother than I ever care to remember. He's been a guy that has been on my side. So, when I now say dad I am referring to my stepfather. He was a chauffeur for Mr. Johnson (one of the originators or owners of newspapers, a rich dap cat). Anyway, Mr. Johnson allowed my dad to have an old Model-A Ford. I remember when he used to date my mom after she had left my biological father and gotten a divorce. They married and my mom and I went to live with him. His wife had died some years earlier, and he is considerably older than my mom. My mom is 56, and my dad is 69, maybe 70. Anyway, at this particular point in time, I sang in a choir and so did Johnson's daughter. We were in high school together and I kind of dug her and she kind of dug me. And being the open and honest kid that she was, she went home and told her parents that she dug this kid. Being the open-minded liberal people that they were, they wanted to know who this fellow was, and she, being the open-minded kid that she was, she told them. And then they said "Oh, no!" They went into their act. I remember Johnson calling my dad. My dad was no longer working for him at that time. The war was on at that time, the Second World War, and both my parents were working at an army installation in Dixon. He called and he rapped to my dad. I understand that your son has been trying to date my daughter, etc., and I think she finds this a little bit upsetting. My dad was very cool with it, you know. My dad said he had not heard me calling her on the phone so much as he had been answering the phone when she had been calling here. This "pissed" the father off like something terrible because his shining star had been doing all this calling. So his next rap was to talk to my mother. He told her that it might be best if she got her son out of here. "Do you have any relatives in Chicago or somewhere?" My mom said yes to that. "I'll pay his bus fare to get the fellow out of town." My mom came and talked to me and I told her yes, I liked Jane, she's nice, and I don't feel like I'm hung up on her or anything. But I don't feel like I'm going to leave town. What's all this business about. It's his daughter and if he has a problem with it let him worry about controlling her. Why are you going to shoot me off to the Sierras or something like that. Anyway we got this worked out. My dad, he was with it. I didn't go out of town. There was not a serious thing with us anyway. We were good friends; I liked her and she liked me. I think as people like people we could talk about things. We enjoyed singing together and things of this sort, nothing sexual. It never got to that point; it could have I suppose if it had gone on, but it didn't. It was just a normal young teenage kind of friendship like any two teenagers could cultivate without knowing all the taboos. I was hurt, angry, and mad, because the issue for me at that point was that this cat was rejecting me because I was black and here he was preaching equality through his writing and all this other kind of business. But when push came down to shove as he thought it was, that his daughter was romantically interested, he wanted to back-track and do his subterranean kind of thing to break it up. But there was nothing to break up. I had never taken her out on a date. You just didn't do that anyhow. We had lunch together at Kresge's, or maybe we had sat down on a curb by the side of the school building, which was on the fringe of downtown, and ate lunch together. That was all there was to it. The cat is damn near blind now and so be it. I don't wish him blindness but it may help him see better.

You hear white people talking of blacks as being paranoid because they say that they can discern discrimination on the part of whites when they encounter them. That's a protective kind of paranoia if it's real. And it's not far off. In legitimate clinical cases of paranoia there's always a kernel of truth in what a person is paranoid about. I think when you feel that you have been beaten down and your parents have said when they have taken you South, "Be careful of saying yes sir, and don't be trying clothes. Drink out of the fountain that says "Colored" and not the one that says "White." Your parents educate you to where you can and can't go and what you can and what you can't do, so that number one, you don't embarrass them or get them in trouble and, number two, so that you learn for yourself that when you're out there fighting that world on your own you can kind of keep yourself clean.

It's a teaching; it's a training. You're walking down the street with your mother at the age of six or seven and it's just like a retarded child or any other child non-retarded, walking with his mother and all of a sudden the light changes and he's holding her hand. She squeezes it and he learns something is wrong. Mom squeezed my hand so I learned she is on guard about these things. So a certain amount of that paranoia, if that's what it is, is protective. It's also damned diagnostic with a hell of a lot of validity to it too. I think that someone may discover that to be able to read affect you don't have to be a psychologist or a social worker or a psychiatrist. You read affect as you encounter it, and as it is directed toward you. It can be a lot of things, but you kind of feel it. Now the person may change in their behavior toward you if later encounters dictate that, you know, but there are times when you can see it in their responses and in their reactions to other people too. But it's like that dog who raises his ears when a strange noise approaches until he finds out what it's all about.

So this business with interracial dating just didn't happen like it happens now. My son dates. I guess the majority of his dates are white, and I'm not particular about that. We've had some calls; he's had some calls by the fathers of some of the girls that he's dated in terms of their objection to his dating. His attitude has been consistent with mine — that his daughter's choice is a problem for him to work out with his daughter not for my son to be doing any wild changes. And no calls to me, absolutely none. When I have said that I wanted to call the father that had called him, my son has asked me not to because he knows the kinds of changes that I go through. In one instance it was my feeling that this cat didn't have anything to be complaining about; if anything, I felt that my son was too good to be dating her to be perfectly honest about it. So what the hell was he bitching and moaning about. I am not the kind of guy who would say to my son, "No you can't date this one, and yes, you can date that one."

I think my father, meaning my stepfather, went to maybe the seventh or eighth grade. My mother went to the third or fourth. They both worked during the time I was in grade school and high school. They didn't know what career lives were. I guess high school was as far as they could see. The bachelor's degree and on forward was a thing that wasn't in their experience to really understand. There was a black physician and a black dentist in the community at that time. I don't think that my mother ever felt that she wanted her son to be a doctor or a lawyer. It wasn't the kind of thing that was discussed with me around a dinner table or things of this sort. It just didn't happen this way. She was just trying to make ends meet. Like I said, my dad was down in a hole, digging streets, and putting in sewers for the WPA, from the time that I was in elementary school until the war started.

There was no conversation in the home concerning educational pursuits. There were no books or other things that were educationally stimulating in the house. My dad could read; my mom could read too. There were magazines at home because before my mother went to work at the army depot she was a domestic. This was one of the ways that I got some of the clothes that I had and she used to bring some magazines home. But my parents didn't go out and buy books for me. If the best-seller was the thing in that day we didn't know a thing about it in our house. I remember at one point there was a black author who was peddling his own books. He sold my parents a copy and autographed it. This was their way of rewarding me for staying in school. Hell, I was in the seventh or eighth grade, and this man didn't mean a thing to me. I read the book. It was an interesting book but no more interesting than the books I was reading at Washington School. I was hung up on Beowolf and the rest of it. So there was not that kind of outside stimulation that was coming in on me. I had no older brothers or sisters who preceded me in school who were exposed to learning. I got what I was getting on my own and bringing it in to my parents rather than vice versa.

My mom would say, "nice report card," or "glad to see you doing okay," or something like that. I can remember that she was so busy working and so tired because she worked so hard cleaning floors. I used to go to PTA chili suppers and all this kind of jazz. I dug this. I took my little can of chili beans to the potluck and mom would say that she couldn't go because she was tired or something. Some nights she had to work; some nights she had been tired. Well, I had been tired too. It kind of hurt me because here I am alone. A number of the other kids were there with me; alone without parents. The majority of parents there were white. There were black parents there too. But still you kind of felt that maybe you were a little different. I don't know, maybe deprived. I don't know how I thought of it in those terms. I know I felt hurt that my parents weren't there. I don't want to couch it in any big terms at this point, in looking back on it. I felt hurt that my parents weren't able to come to the chili suppers so that I could say this is my mom and dad; you know, just like everybody else. She made it to only two or three as I can recall.

I was very social in that sense. I dug going back to school events. My dad worked days and evenings and I could understand. But why wasn't he able to come to the PTA meetings once a month, and the chili suppers once a month, and the Boy Scout meetings once a month? He was too damn busy trying to make money to make sure that I could go to this kind of thing. So it went like this pretty much through elementary school. You pretty much got off that kick after you got into junior high because you were kind of hooking it on your own in seventh, eighth, and ninth grade. Now you get there to junior high and you become a hall guard, and then you become something else, and then if you get on the freshman football or basketball team you kind of become a big man on campus and all this kind of business.

I dug learning to the extent of my ability to learn at that point. I didn't put out; I wasn't drawn out. I was there. I suppose out of my own initiative to learn, I learned. It wasn't until I got into senior high school that I had a teacher or two who were really interested in my learning to the extent to really pull out of me what they discerned that I had. One teacher and I are still very good friends today after some twenty years I guess. Ann, I, and the kids visit with her periodically. She's retired, of course, in her late seventies.

There was not that incentive, not that pushing from home or from older brothers or sisters or things of this sort that can be helpful in terms of learning. You either tried to emulate your peers and their performance because you didn't want to be left on the bottom of the stick or you did it because you had a thirst for it or a talent for it. I really didn't get too concerned about the books until I was in the ninth grade and I didn't really have any career choices at that point. I didn't have in my mind that I wanted to be a physicist, an electrician, or anything at that point. I just wanted to make it on and began to work harder in school. I suppose it was just about too late. I think I graduated 212 out of 425 or something like that. I think I made the upper half by maybe one. But I was trying at that time. This teacher that I was telling you about; she's white, took an interest in me, recognized what she thought to be my ability in English, history, etc., and took it upon herself to get in touch with my parents. She got me a scholarship at Howard University in Washington. I didn't want to go to Howard, not under those circumstances. I would have had to work washing dishes in a residence hall. Here I am an athlete type who had excelled a little bit in sports. I was nothing outstanding but I held my own on the football field and basketball during my sophomore and junior years.

I worked the whole time I was in school. I shined shoes. That was a thing you could do when you weren't doing anything else. You could go to the shoe shine parlor and shine shoes, and make enough money to take your girl out. So I quit all sports after the end of my junior year and just worked as a bus boy at a hotel in Dixon. I made money and bought clothes and went that way. I studied and I was still hitting the books pretty good. I got this scholarship as I've told you to Howard and like that was not my style. I wasn't committed to education or a career. I didn't want to go to Howard and wash dishes in a residence hall to get through school.

The Korean War was going pretty good at this point and a friend of mine said let's go into service. My thought was that the GI Bill was available to veterans of the Korean War. You could volunteer and get your choice of branches, whereas if you got drafted you went where they sent you. So I volunteered and my friend volunteered. We thought the Air Force was an attractive thing. You had to have your birth certificate and many other things to get into the Air Force at that time. It was at this time that I discovered that I was illegitimate. When I wrote off to the county clerk in Tennessee, I found out that my parents weren't married when I was born. At that point black people weren't being born in white hospitals and those were the only kinds of hospitals there in that part of Tennessee. And to tell you the truth, I don't think that I had any really major setback. It didn't cause any adolescent, young adult crisis between me and my mother, none of that. I felt kind of hurt in a small way that she hadn't told me this, but then I can understand why you don't tell a child this I guess. I didn't think too much more about it so I went into the Army, and he went into the Air Force.

I was in the Army three years. I joined so that I could get my own pick of assignment, because if you were drafted then you were going pretty much the way kids are going now — zing, infantry or Vietnam. At that point it was infantry, then Korea. Dig the naivete here — this you've got to get. I heard about the Coast Artillery so I said this means the American coast, it means defending the American coast. This means you don't go overseas. So, I say this is fine and I join the Coast Artillery. I went on to Louisville, Kentucky, and later on to Michigan. I stayed there for a few months, through the winter, 1950-51, and later transferred out to Ft. Lewis, Washington. I spent two full years in the states in the Coast Artillery outfit, and the only coast I was on was at Ft. Lewis. I spent eighteen months out there. The last year of my tour, the whole outfit got sent to Korea. That was in 1952, when they were integrating the armed forces; Mark Clark, Truman, and the whole business. They sent our whole outfit over which was later to be integrated with other white outfits. So I was fortunate in that regard; go to service, spend two full years in the States, go to Korea, and come back home and go to school.

Ann and I got married in November of 1950. We were both eighteen at this point. I went to Louisville, Kentucky, and later to Fort Custer, Michigan. We got married there. She came back home and stayed with her family and I stayed there until I finished basic training. Then I got transferred to Ft. Lewis, Washington. It was an all-black outfit with white officers. She moved out there in the fall a year after we were married. We had to live off base because I was not an NCO. We lived in a little place in a subdivision of Tacoma and had to travel into the base every day, about seventeen miles. She had to cook on a wood-burning stove and all the other kinds of roughing it. We moved onto the base when I made corporal. My first son was born in 1952, but about six or seven weeks after his birth he died of a throat obstruction.

I made rank real fast in the service. I think that I was an SFC by the time I was twenty. I was gun commander and I had two guns; one a 40 mm and one a Quad 50. I stayed in Pusan for about six months and then the order came out to integrate things. But I went from the 32nd AA to the 76th up at Kunsan, which was the airbase where the jet aces were flying out of. We were protecting that damn thing. You couldn't protect it against MIGs. We were flying F-86 Sabre Jets out of there and the Red Chinese had MIG 15's. All you could do was put up a wall of fire power so that your planes could get down. You couldn't hit anything except with that Quad 50 if you picked him up two miles ahead of his flight path. But it was in Pusan that I really got interested in some things.

I encountered this chaplain in Pusan who was very much interested in getting some volunteers to write home and get some parents, relatives, etc., to send some clothes for refugees' children. This is when I really got interested in social work. I began to inquire around. One thing led to another and I began to find out that there were schools for social work and you could do such and such after you finished. You needed a bachelor's degree. When time for me to be discharged came, the battalion commander told me that if I extended my time nine months he was going to promote me to warrant officer. I told him no. I wanted to go to school so I took my discharge and came on home.

I got discharged in September 1953, and I worked in Dixon until the fall of 1954. Then I enrolled at Mason (a small university) in the Liberal Arts program. I majored in Sociology and minored in Psych and Business Administration. I was working fulltime at a manufacturing company in Dixon on the extra board, which meant you worked when you could. During the grain season, which was from June to the end of November, you worked very regularly and then things kind of slacked off because the grain harvest was over and you got laid off for two or three months. During those periods, I worked fulltime at the hotels.

One hotel — well, let me kind of sketch it out for you. I'd go to work at 10:45 at night at the plant, and I'd work until 6:45 in the morning. It would take me until about 7:15 to get down to the hotel where I was the room service breakfast waiter. I took all the room service orders for breakfast, got them up and served them on carts in the rooms. I'd do maybe twelve or fifteen breakfasts at the most; two or three at the least. You were hustling tips and a little bit of salary; ten cents an hour or something like that. Then I would take off and make my 9 o'clock class at Mason. I was in school from 9 o'clock until something like 1 o'clock. Ann's brother and I were in school together. Whoever got out of school first, whichever day it was, had to fix lunch for the both of us. I would come home, eat lunch, and go back. I was carrying a full load in school, between fifteen and seventeen hours. I'd go back to school for probably an hour or two, then go to the hotel, where I was a bell hop. Ann's brother ran the elevator at the hotel. One of her other brothers was the head porter and bartender. I would kiss her, say how are you, how's our boy, he's fine, etc., and see you later. I'd hop bells from maybe two until four or five o'clock, which was pretty much the busiest time when people were checking in. Then I would go home and go to bed at about five or six o'clock and sleep until ten o'clock and then get up and make it back to the plant at 10:45. It was that kind of thing through four years in college.

I graduated from high school with maybe a weakish kind of C average, but every other semester I was on the honor roll at Mason.

But that kind of push was an internal kind of thing. I had to do this three-job business. I think the first couple of semesters I really surprised myself. I had no idea of what kind of job I was going to get when I got out of Mason. I decided at that point to go to grad school. Well, I had decided before then, because I wanted to become a social worker. My professor of sociology wanted me to enroll in the University of Illinois or Washington University of St. Louis. But the only place that I wanted to go was the University of Chicago and I wrote there. They looked at my undergraduate record, and asked what are you going to do about money. I said I didn't know. I've got two years left of my GI Bill, and I said what can one do about money? Can I work? And they said you can work no more than ten hours a week. So I said I would work ten hours a week. But, what can you earn working ten hours a week? She told me about some scholarships, competitive scholarships that were available through the State of Illinois Department of Mental Health. I went and took the exams and won one and that is how I got through graduate school. The state puts you through two years of school or whatever your graduate education is and you pay them back in terms of time. I graduated from the University of Chicago and I went to work as a social worker. I had intentions of going to California, but I dug the experience that I had clinically and professionally so much that I stayed with it. Later I went into private practice, counselling and psycho-therapy and, well, three years ago we bought a house.

Private practice has always been a sideline with me; it's a thing that I've enjoyed. That's not the major thing that I do. I started out as a clinical psychiatric social worker, and worked up to being a supervisor at the administrative level.

I deal with severely emotionally disturbed kids and mentally re-tarded children. I've been in private practice which started out as a ten hour kind of thing and it's dwindled down to maybe about four or five hours a week now. It's a thing I enjoy, more of a sideline.

Personally, I'm a non-belonger to a lot of groups. I'm very active in community affairs, however, which doesn't require belonging to groups you know. I have a lot of commitment to this town. I've had this interest since I got out of school. I was one of the first people involved in a demonstration against a chain store and I brought my wife and kids into it too. Those interests have sustained themselves on my part in a very active fashion over the years. Someone asked me the other day how I keep my name out of the paper and I said, well, if you don't make news you don't get your name in the paper. My bag is not to make news or to present myself as a leader because I don't see myself as that. The majority of my private clientele, meaning paying clientele, are the children of professional people or couples from the upper level of society in this community. My colleagues are from similar levels; others are not you know. I travel in that white socioeconomic professional structure of the community. My own interests lead me to be involved in lower social economic structure, so that I have contacts with just about all levels of people in the community, socially and professionally.

I worked for the Cook County Public Aid Office in Chicago. I would say that 50 percent of my clients in my field placement in the Public Aid Department were black. I would say that another 30 percent were Mexican-American; another 20 percent were white. Social relationships were mixed. You had the body of your student colleagues and the parties and the after-school beers and the whole bit at the University Tap and Jimmy's. I have relatives in Chicago and my wife has relatives in Chicago. We were included in that segment of it too. Among these were redcaps at the train stations, skycaps at the airports, and owners of small businesses. It was a mixed crowd too so that we enjoyed the best.

But you know I think that my own liking for people came from the fact that I grew up in a "ghetto" as much as you can describe a central midwest town as having a "ghetto." I think in its own way it's a real division of people and a concentration of poverty and problems and everything else. This is why I always say ghetto in quotes because I think it is a peculiar kind of term. I can't say truthfully that any part of my drive has been a reaction to necessarily being discriminated against. How do you know whether it's hurt you or not? How can you tell? If you asked me, if it beat down my personality or my drive or something else I would have to say no. If you ask me if it made it stronger, I'd probably have to say yes in some ways that I can't really define. All the times that I felt somebody was shooting darts into me might have made me stronger. But now I don't know. I think when you are over at the manufacturing plant pulling corn with an electric shovel out of a boxcar and have gotten dust in your lungs and in your nose, that's the thing that you detest.

People at that point didn't just openly call you derogatory names and things of this sort. Even if they did, I think I was much more prone to defend myself against that kind of action. But even the notion that you had to sit in the balcony instead of the first floor, didn't bug me. That wasn't the impetus to my wanting to better myself you know, if this was the issue. That wasn't it. It was the feeling that I didn't want to stand down in that ditch and dig those holes for the rest of my life out in the cold like it is now. I didn't dig that. I didn't want to be out there pounding spikes in the cross-ties and straightening rails during the hot summer and the cold winter, which I was doing sometimes. I didn't want to always be standing up serving this cat his food you know for the rest of my life. I wanted at some point to have someone serve some food to me in a nice place. But I can't say that as a result, as a direct result or a direct function of my having been discriminated against, a personal insult and all the other kinds of things, that this was the main driving force for me in getting an education and doing some other things. The point was, how can you escape from the drudgery, personal, economic and otherwise, that you had to contend with? How do you escape from this? And the cats would say, man, what in the hell are you going to college for? You know, what's this all about? You can't be a this, you can't be a that, you can't be the other and all this kind of business. The thing that I'm saying is well maybe no, not right now.

But what gets alarming about this is that you get to graduate school in Chicago and you take a Christmas job between your first and second quarter at the Chicago Post Office. There's some lawyers there and they are in there pitching this mail right in there with you. And why are they there? Because they don't have access to law firms. Their wife is working and they are working at the post office. They are chasing ambulances and a number of other things trying to get a stake so that they can go into their own thing you know. That frightens you. It really frightens you when you are in the company of cats that have achieved education and haven't been able to use it.

I didn't dig the drudgery of work you know; this old 6:45 in the morning out in the cold business. I wanted a desk job. I wanted to use the head too, because I discovered I had one too. I didn't like the drudgery. I saw it in my mother's experience. She didn't have a stick mop to wax floors with, she had to do it on her knees. And even though I've been able to buy her much hand lotion and knee lotions, and she's been able to buy them herself in later years, the marks are still there — still there. The identification with the drudgery and the way she had to hustle and the way my dad had to hustle to support the three of us got to me. Even my working and hustling my own clothes to take the load off of them told me I didn't want this. It wasn't being called "nigger" by some white cats that said that you had to go out there and get your letters so you can do your thing. That wasn't it. It's being down in that system saying that you've got to go down and dig the ditches because you don't have the education, a high school diploma which was the thing. Or you have to shine the shoes, you have to bus the dishes, you have to wait the tables which I thoroughly enjoyed. I dug waiting tables. I loved to meet people. I met a lot of celebrities, but it still wasn't what I wanted to do the rest of my life.

Well, I want my kids to want something better for themselves. I try to expose them to something better for themselves. When I say this I don't mean that I'm trying to encourage what I consider to be false values in my kids. All I'm saying is that there are some worlds to be achieved out here that I haven't and they can if they want to. I'm not trying to put things out of their reach in terms of how they measure their capacity against achievement. I just want to expose them to things and teach them how to make up their own minds about what they want; what's vital and what's necessary. I'm friends with my kids. My wife is very much a friend with our children. I'm a stern, strict kind of guy and I set limits. But I'm also a friend. My son and I, we share some kind of interest and we indulge it. We play golf and we do all kinds of things together. My son likes nice things just like I do and he doesn't dig all the drudgery either. He's a kid that's caught up in black aware-ness. I was social protesting at his age too, as I've said before, when it was very unpopular to be that way in the community. I support his activities but at the same time I let him know that I support the system in the sense that he has to suffer the consequences of his actions. This means that if you are going to boycott over here at the high school and you know what the consequences of boycotting are, I support your boy-cotting, but you take the consequences. He's known for a number of years that I'm very much involved in civil rights activities and always have been. I've taken him to some things with me. When he was eight I had him walking the picket line. I want him to be involved. I want him to be concerned. I want him to be aware. He does some things that I disapprove of as far as how the protest expresses itself. But I don't stop him from protesting in his own way.

He's a pretty together guy. What I mean by that is he is at school, he's with things, he takes care of his things around the house here for the most part. We have normal parent-adolescent housekeeping prob-lems around here like any normal family does. The same way with my daughter. She's much fonder of the books than he is, but I don't knock him. I try to expose him, I try to provide things for him, I take the horse to water is what I'm saying. He is a young man now, and I play it kind of loose with him in that sense. There are some things that I'm very stern and firm about. When the kids buck the limit, I have to really sit down and say no dice, no good, and we get along from there.

But those times are few and far between. Sometimes he and I have a real hard conflict about something, whether it's dating, whether it's demonstrations over there at the high school, or whatever. He doesn't venture that far outside of what's acceptable to me, and maybe it's because I identify very much with what he's doing and why I feel he needs to be doing some of the things. But at the same time, I support the school. It's kind of hard for him. Because here he is a black high school senior, living in this community with the kinds of problems that are going on over there in that high school with gangs and everything else operating around here. He doesn't belong to a gang, but part of that is because he is basically inaccessible to the gang from a residential standpoint. The other part is because he's a personable guy and he relates easily to kids on both sides of the fence. I can't say that he's learned that from me. He has it in his own right. He does make snap judgments but he's able to recall them. He relates to a person for what he is and who he is without being a black snob. I would detest it if I thought he were.

I only consider myself middle class by others' definitions of middle class. I may be middle class by economic and educational definitions. Housing-wise I may be middle class. I don't consider myself by way of identification, self-identity as being middle class. That is not where my loyalty lies. I have learned to speak with the middle class and with the upper class in their own terms. But by virtue of whatever I've achieved educationally and economically I have not lost, nor have I sought to lose, my ability to relate, to actively be interested in and involved with, what you might call the lower class. You can come in this house on any given time that I'm having a party and you will find people, for the most part, from all social strata. You'll find some mail-carriers here. You won't know they are mail-carriers unless you are a person, one of these middle-class types, who asks questions about what do you do. Some people have to define themselves in terms of knowing what someone else does. It's like the gal at the checkout counter who was very much interested in knowing what my wife did. She presumed what she did and asked are you a teacher? Ann said no and finished with my groceries. Is your husband a minister? "No, he's not; sack up my groceries." But people have to pigeon-hole you somehow in order it seems for them to relate to you. I don't go through life that way. I don't give a damn what you do. I think I'm a social historian; this is my training. I'm a clinician, but what does it matter, because if I can dig you as a person, you can take the rest of it and junk it, really. There are some people that really get turned off unless they know what you do. They have to, black and white people, not just white. But I don't consider myself middle class except in terms of how some people feel that they must identify me somehow in order to relate to me.

Discussion

In the categories of our typology it is clear that Robert Black is a Benevolent. His inter- and intraracial tolerance is attested to by his disregard for class, status or race factors in determining social relationships for himself and his family. He actively participates in civil rights activities and encourages and supports his son's protest activities. He is fairly militant in his efforts at black protest but far from radical.

Robert Black has experienced considerable social mobility, yet it is important to note that his point of departure was not from the lowest rung on the black social ladder. His parents were stably employed, his housing conditions were good and he achieved an adequate education in the public schools. His early family life, although marred a bit by divorce and death, was basically sound, stable, and supportive. The church, which seems to have failed in imparting its dogma and ritual to Mr. Black, succeeded very well in providing him with healthy and non-destructive peer social relationships, one of which turned out to be his life mate.

Racial prejudice and discrimination have played a dominant role in the life of this man, yet taken as a whole they have not embittered him toward whites or turned him against black people. Although he was raised under conditions of partial segregation, the color line was not absolute. He encountered racial slums and attacks in sports but excelled in spite of them. The negative effect of his relationship with the white girl in school was somewhat muted by the support he received from his family. His advancement in the Army was not impeded by his color and he actually first discovered his calling while in the service. When he recounted his work experience while in college, he emphasized the nature of physical labor as being more oppressive than the fact that he was a black man working for whites. Even his recent experience with the child who called him "'nigger" seemed to evolve more a feeling of pity for the child and mother than hostility.

Without discounting the factors of his own internal strength and confidence in himself, derived from his education and work experience, it seems that the support Robert Black received from his parents, his father-in-law, and his own family explains in large part how he maintains such a positive inter- and intraracial stance.

7

Summary

and

Conclusions

The purpose of this study has been to analyze and describe the basic character of the black middle class, a group of people who have ascended to an important position in the interracial life of the United States. The major thrust of this effort has been to address the question: What is the black middle class like in the third quarter of the twentieth century? To this end, we have focused our analysis on three central propositions about this group. What now can we say about the validity of these propositions in light of the evidence presented?

Evidence on the Propositions

The first proposition was that, taken as a whole, the black middle class of the 1960s and 1970s represents a group of striving, responsible citizens and does not conform well to the irresponsible, "aping of whites" description given to them in the past. From the data presented in Chapter 2, it is clear that this proposition is strongly supported. Rather than an image of moderately well-off white-collar workers trying to live a life style attributable to the upper-class, aristocratic elements in the white community (Frazier 1962, p. 169), we find a group of individuals living within their means and striving to carve out a life without ostentatiousness and pretense. They are highly family-oriented in terms of their marriage and remarriage rate, small family size, and propensity to spend their leisure time in family-centered activities. They live the bulk of their lives outside of the sphere of work, almost totally within the confines of the black community, and they prefer black people over whites for social interaction. As a group, they are not afraid to compete with whites at work and, in some cases, welcome the challenge (recall Robert Black's description of the role that competition with whites played in his life). Coupled with minimal interracial contact is the theme of racial responsibility, evidenced by a high degree of involvement in civil rights, independent political action, and a strain of group self-hatred caused by the feeling that middle-class blacks have not done enough to assume leadership and advance their race. Withdrawal to the confines of just the middle-class black community and self-imposed isolation from the problems of the black masses is no longer a major goal for the middle-class black man as it was in earlier decades. Instead, a fairly militant positive-activist racial stance is the norm and is considered a status-enhancing endeavor.

The second proposition posited that the black middle class has developed and differentiated structurally to the point that no longer should a black man be defined as middle-class on the basis of having some public schooling and a stable income-producing occupation. A true discernable black middle class has emerged. American society now includes an identifiiable group of genuinely middle-class blacks: college-educated individuals with white-collar occupations who are distinct in many ways from the stably employed blue-collar, working-class. It is much too crude at this point in time to consider mailmen and pullman porters in the same social category as pharmacists, attorneys, and physicians, for there are major differences in their cultural life styles, political attitudes, and racial stance, as well as a major gap in their socioeconomic status. The data in Chapter 3 support this contention for the individuals sampled in one neighborhood and in one city.

The third proposition was that the black middle class can be differentiated into analytic types with distinct behavioral and attitudinal patterns along the dimensions of interracial and intraracial attitudes. Four fairly distinct types were distinguished along these dimensions:

1. *Benevolents*:   Inter- and intraracially tolerant individuals, who tended to be young, socially stable, militant, and civil rights participators.

2. *Uncle Toms*:   Pro-white and anti-black individuals, who tended to be older and socially mobile in terms of occupation.

3. *Race Men*:   Pro-black and anti-white individuals, who were the most darkly colored, least edu-

cated, and the most likely to have been born
and raised in a Northern environment.

4. *World Haters*: Anti-white and anti-black individuals, who
were older and socially stable, and held the
highest socioeconomic status positions in the
sample.

We find that the majority of the younger individuals are the most
positively disposed toward both races (keeping in mind that anti-white
hostility is the norm for all types and differs only in degree). The remainder of the younger people are definitely anti-white in orientation.
As the life process unfolds, especially through geographic movement and
encounters with racial discrimination, it seems that individuals of this
class become more hostile toward whites. Many also seem to become
hostile toward their own race and become either Uncle Toms or World
Haters. The outcome seems dependent upon occupational mobility and
status. The Race Men's position is highly related to darker skin coloring,
which in a very graphic sense forces high racial identification and concomitant black chauvinism. Negative feelings toward the white majority
group is highly related to heavy alcohol consumption and somatic and
physiological symptoms of stress.

Generalizability of the Findings

We have asserted that we are studying the black middle class. However,
we have but eighty lengthy interviews, taken from respondents in and
around one community area of Chicago. Further, the bulk of our analysis
deals with only sixty of the interviews. One could ask not only about the
generalizability of these data but whether they can be generalized.

Our answer to such questions is, first, that certainly the sample
size is small, but it does cover almost the total range of occupations
and age distribution in the white-collar black population. This is something no other in-depth survey research has done to date. Furthermore,
although the respondents are clustered in and around a single community
area, validation that this group exemplifies the essence of the black middle class in Chicago and is in most respects truly representative of this
class is given by the informed opinion of black elites which will be presented in the next section. Briefly, they all agreed with the major conclusions of this study and felt that these conclusions were for the most
part applicable to all urban middle-class blacks. Secondly, we would
argue that the focus of this analysis was on change and differentiation

and that to find this in a small and clustered number of cases indicates
that it truly exists.

A View From the Top

Presented next is a composite perspective on the black middle class
given by five leaders of the black community of Chicago representing the
professional, business, educational, and religious segments of the community. These men were interviewed after the first six chapters were
completed so that the results could be discussed with them.[1]

Perhaps the most important contribution that these individuals have
made to this study is their agreement with the findings. The only point on
which they took issue was the apparent high degree of identification and
involvement of the sample as a whole with the civil rights movement. The
elites feel that this conclusion slightly overstates the case and that, by and
large, the middle class is quite conservative in their support of the movement. They generally asserted that the residents of Chatham were typical
of middle-class black people who reside in the other large concentrations
of higher income black persons in the Lake Meadows-Prairie Shores
housing areas and at the peripheries of the lower-class housing areas on
the South Side, such as South Shore and Avalon Park. On the other hand,
it was pointed out to the author that there was little similarity between
the middle classes who live in the just mentioned areas and those who
reside in the Hyde Park-Kenwood community areas of Chicago. Here, it
was generally felt, is where the upper-middle and upper-class black families are concentrated. Their incomes tend to be above $25,000 per year,
and they tend to be in the higher echelons of their professions. For example, the Johnsons of Johnson Publications live in Kenwood. And although
there are attorneys and businessmen in Chatham and Lake Meadows, the
senior partners and high-level managers of firms live in Kenwood and
Hyde Park. It was also indicated that this area is the residential base of
the social and intellectual elites of the black community. They have their
own social networks and "social sets," live a much higher style of life
than do the Chatham residents, and move in different social circles,

---

[1]The author had sent out letters to twelve prominent individuals in the hope of
interviewing them all and using this material as a separate chapter. The five reported
here are the results of that enterprise. Needless to say, there was considerable reticence on the part of the black leadership to share their views. Whether this reticence
was due to the author's university affiliation or to the sensitive nature of the subject
is not known for certain. However, I feel that the latter is the case.

although they may interact with middle-class black people in the occupational sphere.

In the view of the elite informants, members of the black middle class are conservative and are "just trying to make it." They are insecure and anxious about their status and their primary concern is with carving out a life for themselves and their families. The informants feel that those with Southern socialization, Southern college education, and a non-middle-class background tend to be at the forefront of this type of conservatism. Unlike the Northern-socialized black man or the second generation professional or white-collar worker who is accustomed to middle-class status and is not fearful of losing it, these who are mobile, either geographically or occupationally, are afraid and devote their energies more to solidifying their positions than to concerning themselves with problems faced by the black lower class. Even Robert Black did not want to make "headlines." Yet they identify with black people generally and with other middle-class blacks. Also, they are not too concerned with entry into the white community; rather, they want to establish their own community apart from the whites and apart from the black lower class. They desire nice homes and good schools for their children, and for these reasons they move into white areas of the city. But they do not have to be integrated with whites per se. Nevertheless, the presence of whites usually means that the schools will be better and the community services adequate.

On the other hand, the presence of the black lower class usually means that the personal safety of the families of the black middle class is threatened and that the quality of the schools is threatened. Hence, fear of the black lower class pervades this group. They are not disparaging of lower-class blacks, for they feel it is not the latter's fault that these conditions exist, but they do fear them. This is a major problem; for the elites as well as the author feel that at the very time when racial identification is increasing among the black middle class, the gap between this group and the lower class is increasing. The middle class is no longer able to understand and empathize fully with black masses; sympathize, yes, but empathize, no.

This situation has profound implications for the development and recruitment of leadership and guidance for the black lower class. The elites are quite dismayed by the reticence of members of the middle class to assume leadership, and they envisage with horror a situation in which the recruitment of leaders for the masses comes from the poorly educated and unskilled members of the masses themselves. Needless to say, radicalism in race relations does not find support to any great extent in the upper classes either.

Another major contribution of this elite perspective is the notion that the middle class of the black community has not changed as much as the author had envisioned. There was agreement that the legal, political, and economic gains of the last decade have had a pronounced effect upon the black middle class in the form of greater commitment to racial problems. However, there was great consensus that Frazier overstated his case concerning the snobbery and falseness of life of this group. First, it was pointed out that Frazier's greatest acquaintance with middle-class life was centered around the very status-conscious society of Washington, D.C., where, as one member who was a close friend of Frazier's put it, "if you couldn't trace your ancestors back to 1619, no matter how much money you had or how high your position, you were out of it; you were not accepted." Thus, a pullman porter or a clerk could receive deference over a physician or lawyer because of his "heritage" and lineage back to the 1600s. This person also conceded that Chicago had some of this element but not nearly to the extent of Washington. Another elite member reinforced this view by asserting that Chicago has always been the most wide open city in the United States for black people, economically and socially. It is in Chicago where manufacturing, food processing, banking, insurance, and even real estate enterprises owned and operated by black persons have provided the greatest opportunity for qualified black people to work and get ahead in life.

According to one elite, middle-class blacks in Chicago have always worked for the black man's rights, although not to the extent that they do in the context of civil rights today. He spoke of the period during the thirties and forties when the motto, "Don't buy where you can't work," was dominant, and he noted that physicians and lawyers marched right alongside of the unemployed.

Another finding of ours that was clarified by these individuals was the low rates of fraternal and social club membership and participation by our sample. It seems that, in general, separate black institutions and organizations are on the decline. This trend is definitely traceable to the opportunity that qualified black men now have to join white organizations and to travel and move freely in entertainment and dining establishments. Previously, if an individual wanted to eat out, go dancing, or hold a large party, he usually did it in the context of a black organization formed to provide for that purpose. Hence the proliferation of fraternal organizations and social clubs described by Drake and Cayton and Franklin Frazier. Today these restrictions have been lifted and black people with the money and the inclination can obtain services and facilities from the white community. Many have withdrawn from all-black social organizations, some of which have disappeared.

The same process is operative in professional and business organizations. The Dearborn Real Estate Board was formed because the comparable white organization would not allow black men to join; today it does. The Cook County Bar Association is no longer closed to black attorneys. In response to these changes the black organizations have either disbanded or integrated themselves. A good example of this integration is the Cosmopolitan Chamber of Commerce which until 1954 (the year of the famous Supreme Court decision) was an all-black institution. In that year a new executive director was elected whose philosophy was that economic security for the blacks could not be gained through segregation and an appeal to black people to "Buy Black." The reasoning behind this thinking was quite clear. Middle-class black families want quality and low prices, and separate enterprises without the knowledge, skills, and contacts of the white community could not provide this. Therefore, the Cosmopolitan Chamber of Commerce ceased to be an all-black organization and integrated itself with the business and professional interests of the city as a whole. Since doing this, it has prospered a great deal.

Perhaps more notable in this phenomenon of general decline of black institutions has been the decline of the all-black church. The reasons just mentioned explain part of this decline, for the black church as a separate institution provided a framework for business and social activity as well as a context for civil rights activity. Today other organizations have taken over these roles. In addition, in the past as well as now, the Catholic and Episcopal churches have attracted middle-class blacks because they have schools which are generally of better quality than those accessible in the public sphere. In the past it was necessary for the parents to be members of the church or to take instruction if they were not members so that their children could qualify for admittance. Today this qualification is no longer mandatory.

George C. Homans, in his work on the elementary forms of social behavior, presents several propositions that generally apply to relationships of human exchange. The fourth of these propositions states that "the more often a man in the recent past received a rewarding activity from another, the less valuable any further unit of that activity becomes to him" (Homans 1961, p. 55). This seems to be the explanation given by the elites for the minimal amounts of contact with whites outside the arena of work. If a middle-class black man works every day with whites, then additional amounts of contact are worth less and not extremely desirable. With only business and occupational interests in common, blacks and whites terminate contact when all the interaction needed to conclude such business is over. Contact tends to be more frequent and intimate outside the sphere of work if and only if there are other areas of mutual interest. These can be interests in particular sports or other leisure time pursuits mutually shared by both white and black alike. If shared interests are present, off-the-job interracial contacts usually follow and in many cases strong friendships result. If they are not, it is unlikely that the black man will attempt such contact just for the sake of being in white company.

Conclusions

It is apparent that the structure and composition of the middle class is very different today than it was during the period of the 1930s through the early 1950s when Frazier and others did their work. The last decade and a half have produced a true black elite as well as a distinct middle class. The elite is no longer composed only of a handful of successful entrepreneurs and sports and entertainment figures, but it includes an expanding number of executives, educators, and government employees, both elected and appointed, who are integrated into the commercial and political mainstream of American life. This movement may be considered by some as "tokenism," but if it is, it is a degree of tokenism never before witnessed, even during Reconstruction.

More basic to our thesis is the rise and emergence of a significant black middle class. No longer is it composed of descendants of the landed aristocracy mixed with successful mailmen and well-paid manual laborers. Today the middle class is comprised of non-manual service and professional workers employed in tertiary industries. It is highly infused with what Frazier termed the "folk elements," darker colored, occupationally mobile individuals who have altered its basic character; witness Robert Black. This class is less integrated into white society than the upper class and seems to be content with a middle-class way of life, somewhat separate and apart from white America.

Separate from this group in many ways is the stably-employed black working class whose occupational base lies in the manual trades, both skilled and unskilled. Through the security of their positions and the elements of value patterns shared with the middle class, they provide the base from which the next generation and socially mobile middle-class black persons will come. Finally, at the broad base of this class pyramid is the black lower class, constrained to a desperate position in the ghettos of the large cities in the United States. The deplorable condition of their life style coupled with their slim hope that these conditions will be alleviated leads them directly into the hate-based black chauvinistic movements. These movements, incidentally, may serve a very useful function in socializing personally disorganized individuals into the middle-class ethics of work and responsibility.

Internal Differentiation and Its Relationship to Interracial Sentiments

As a whole, the black middle class has no powerful motivation for courting the white community. Interracial contact with whites outside the sphere of work is minimal, as is the desire for more intense contact. Nevertheless, there are differences along this dimension which we are now in a position to explore.

First, we will deal with the most integrative section in the black community — the social and intellectual elites and the older, socially stable, high-status elements of the black middle class. These groups are now and have been at the top of the black status hierarchy, and the challenge for them is entrance into the white world. They have little status anxiety within their own community and hold social and cultural values in common with whites. They have suffered the least amount of discrimination and those who have experienced discrimination or thought that they have, have mellowed and accepted it as a thing of the past. Their basis for common value orientations is bifurcated according to racial characteristics and consequent differing feelings about being black and black cultural heritage.

For the stable, light-colored sector, African heritage like any form of ascription is a thing to be played down. Their theme is one of achievement and of present position in society. They feel that their success in a competitive situation is not unlike that of similarly situated whites, and with their comparable style of life they feel that they should have links with people like themselves in the white community. In this context, race is to be ignored as an element not to be considered. The light-colored, old line middle class are the most prone to ignore or at least not to participate in the movement.

For the darker-colored sector, the factor of race and cultural heritage is crucial. They feel it necessary for their self-esteem that the white man note and respect their physical and cultural differences just as they are expected to do the same for whites. Their view is that only if the white man will first accept them as racially different with a culture and history of which they can be proud will they accept the white man and respect his culture and history. In other words, the black man says: "We are different. Respect these differences and then we will interact over the interests which we have in common." The common interests are, of course, those of life style and similar status position in society. These people, although they emphasize racial differences, are most accepting of interracial marriage and are the most positively disposed toward the black lower class. They are also the least conservative in the realm of militancy and civil rights activity.

As our findings illustrate, the black middle class is being infused with elements quite dissimilar to the aforementioned groups. Today, younger and socially mobile individuals are flowing into the black middle class who are quite militant about the status of their people and little concerned with interaction within the white community. Their base is primarily found in northern cities where they have suffered neither a great deal of discrimination (in fact, discrimination in reverse seems to be operating today) nor the punitiveness of Southern experience. However, they are conservative in that they seek to remain within the confines of their own community.

In summary, then, we can state that the processes of economic and social differentiation are active in the middle-class community. These processes, coupled with the changing nature of the environment of the middle-class black (residence in better residential areas of northern cities), and infused with a traceable impact of the civil rights movement such as race pride and non-acceptance of whites primarily for prestige-gaining reasons, has produced an image of this group quite different from that of the black bourgeoisie. Elements of the bourgeoisie still remain, it is true, but their dominance has declined and their place is quickly being taken over by individuals who conform much more closely to the New Negro image.

Psychological and Sociological Perspectives

The first and major premise that E. Franklin Frazier set forth about the psychology and social psychology of the black middle class was that their ultimate goal was to live socially like whites and to be accepted socially by them. "Whiteness," social acceptance, and social interaction with whites outside the spheres of occupational competition and personal competence were their obsession. The struggle for the status that came from socializing with whites was their all-consuming desire. From this premise, Frazier argued, followed the fact that the middle class almost totally lacked identification with the black man, his tradition, and his culture. From the white community's rejection of his attempts followed the frustrations and consequent loss of identity and falseness of life.

A simplified description of this in the language of Allport and Horney would be that, as a whole, this class of a minority group had moved *toward* the oppressor, had been rejected, and had reacted to that rejection extropunitively. The extropunitive reaction comes from the fact that the middle class felt that their rejection was due to the stigma of being black which was perpetuated by the black lower class. Therefore, they blamed their rejection by whites on the black lower class and turned away from the lower-class black man in disgust.

The data that we have presented on this aspect of the black middle class indicate that this premise of Frazier's and his line of reasoning that follows are questionable for the black middle class of today. The minimal amount of social integration with the white community evidenced by this group supports the contention that they have been rejected — or does it? Rejection implies the thwarting of some volitional action. From the responses received regarding desired social contact with whites, it appears that the motivation is lacking in the first place. In other words, the majority of the middle-class respondents do not desire greater amounts of contact and integration with whites and in many instances indicate that the present level of contact is too much.

Therefore, we would argue that Frazier's major premise is no longer applicable to the bulk of the black middle class. We do not contend that Frazier was in error, for from comments given by the elites interviewed, it seems that his assertion was very valid for a description of the highly circumscribed middle- and upper-class communities centered in Washington, D. C., around black southern colleges, and to a lesser extent, of the black "society of Chicago some twenty or thirty years ago." In fact, after talking to a number of middle-class black families as well as to the elites, it is the author's opinion that Frazier's *Black Bourgeoisie* was a very close approximation of the life style of the black middle class of this nation as it existed before the civil rights movement. His book characterized the dominant theme or the statistical majority mode of life of this group. In other words, he was talking about the dominant social type of the black middle class — the black bourgeoisie. He neglected to speak of other less prevalent social types that existed for that was not his goal. Our findings merely indicate that the dominant social type of today in the black middle class is no longer the black bourgeoisie but the New Negro or the New Black Man.

Therefore, today we would argue that a more valid premise to start from is that middle-class black people are most concerned with developing a community of their own apart from the black lower class and that, because of the conditions of housing and school facilities, they must of necessity have some proximity to white communities, but this is not a value in and of itself. Rather, they are willing to compete with the white man occupationally and accept the serious and responsible attitude toward life that he does, but have little motivation to move in his social circles, interact with him just because he is white, or "ape" him in exaggerated forms of leisure time and consumption behavior. Their aping seems to be applicable only to the extent that they take their work seriously and are highly family-centered.

It seems that middle-class blacks are attempting to move away from the oppressor, not in a nationalistic, separatist sense, but more in terms of a personal desire to be given the opportunity to develop themselves and prove themselves worthy of respect within the confines of their own community. The evidence for this is weak but consistent over our sample. The materials in Chapters 4, 5 and 6, in an illustrative manner, bear directly on this problem.

Implications for the Future

With the emergence of a distinct black middle class, the middle-class black man is beginning to redefine himself in relation not only to the larger white community but to his race and to his traditions. Real progress has been made, predominately in the legal sphere, but also in the world of work and social opportunity as well. The middle-class black man now defines himself as "the man of the hour" and must realistically place the burden of the implementation of legal opportunities directly upon himself. This is a difficult position in that he feels he must please two masters, two conflicting demands. He must achieve and live a style of life that will gain for himself and his people in general the respect and acceptance of the white community. In the competitive world of twentieth-century America, this is clearly a full-time pursuit. On the other hand, he feels that he must serve the interests of his race and his people by providing the leadership and guidance necessary to help alleviate the condition of the majority of blacks in the United States. This task also requires a great deal of time, energy, and sacrifice; it is more than a full-time job. It is on the horns of this dilemma that the middle-class black man rests.

To serve his own interests and those of his family is to lead a model life and to conform or even over-conform to the Protestant ethic standards of our society. Acting in this way would achieve the respect of the white community, thereby gaining entry into the larger society for more of his people. But to follow this path would provoke the condemnation of the black lower class (witness the distrust of middle-class elements in the more militant civil rights groups such as SNCC and CORE) who need their leadership and political skills.

The middle-class black man's alternative is to plunge headlong into the battle for civil rights implementation and to gain the support of black people. But, by doing so, he would have to sacrifice the material and social comforts of life for himself and his family. In fact, one could make the case that not only would comforts be sacrificed but also perhaps the educational and occupational futures of his children — a steep price to pay for any individual.

It is evident in the past that personal self-interest has been the norm among middle-class blacks as among middle-class whites. It is clear today that personal self-interest is a pervading force within this group. The very conservatism of their effort coupled with the rampant demand on the part of the black lower class to be given access to some of the opportunities and benefits of our society has led to an increasing estrangement between the middle- and the lower-class masses. The middle-class black feels an ever-increasing identification with his race in general, but at the same time fears that the scope and immensity of the problems of the lower class preclude solution in the foreseeable future. This feeling gives rise to the fear that encroachment by the lower class may destroy the life that he had made for himself and the gains in the image of the blacks that he has presented to the white community. In a sense, the emergence and the entrenchment of the black middle class today has increased the social and psychological distance between themselves and the black lower class. Their life chances are almost incomparable today.

It is interesting and even distressing to note that environmental change has operated in two directions. It has increased the awareness of the middle-class black man to the plight of his race and given him greater positive identification as being black. Yet at the same time it has lifted him higher socially and economically, away from the majority of his people.

But now, what can we say concerning the future of race relations and the role played in them by the black middle class? It is our opinion that events will change, not in kind, but rather in degree. The middle class will continue to differentiate and expand, but in so doing it will tend more to solidify its position and to become much more class conscious. The infusion of more and more socially mobile individuals may add to the conservative trend.

This trend toward conservatism must be accepted with caution, however. When we speak of the conservative middle-class black man, we must remember that we are talking about a group of blacks who have evidenced political independence from the Democratic political organization, participated in and lent financial support to the civil rights movement, and as a group have no great liking or desire to interact a great deal with whites. Their life style as a whole is conservative, as is their support for civil rights, in that there are few outspoken and overly committed individuals recruited from the black middle class. Yet the environment is changing; and although we have argued that our analytic types are closely tied to age and life cycle, the environment is becoming increasingly supportive of racial self-determination and acceptance of the black man. Therefore, it is very likely that some Benevolents and the Race Men category will not move toward other positions but will retain their inter- and intraracial dispositions throughout their lifetimes.

In addition, it is apparent that social mobility is not solely confined to the movement from blue-collar or working-class status to middle-class status. An ever-increasing social and intellectual elite will develop from the middle-class base. It is from within these status-safe groups and from the indigenous elements of the lower class that the leadership of the civil rights movement of the future will be drawn. It is these individuals, deeply concerned with racial pride, cultural heritage, and even black power, who will force the implementation of legal civil rights gains. This is much the same pattern evidenced by earlier European ethnic groups in which the status-safe elites and the grass roots, popularly supported elements, took over leadership.

However, there are few new migrants to urban America to help push the black man up the social ladder; and, given the immensity of the problem, unless there is a tremendous supportive effort on the part of white Americans, it is not unreasonable to assume that the condition of lower-class black people will not change much in the coming decades. Nevertheless, the trend seems to be that the middle class will provide the model of the acceptable black man, although it is from outside this group that leadership must come. This is not to say that the middle class will not support the movement, for they surely will. They will support it for reasons of self-esteem and race pride as well as for the very obvious practical reason that they are the prime beneficiaries of civil rights gains. They have been the beneficiaries up until now, and there is no reason to believe that they will not be in the future.

Appendix A

The Questionnaire

1. First of all, we would like to know what people expect and aspire to in life. Here are some things that different people may expect to attain in their lives. GIVE RESPONDENT PAGE A (See p. 162).

   a. In column one would you please check off the ones that *you already achieved.*

   b. Now in column two would you please check off the ones that *you* wanted very much when *you were younger.*

   c. In column three would you check off the ones that *you still desire* and *have not yet achieved.*

   d. Finally, in column four would you check off those that you *want very much for your child.*

2. Now we would like to get some idea of whether or not you are involved in voluntary organizations. Do you belong to any voluntary organizations like fraternal, church, veteran's, civic, sports, or professional organizations?

Name	Are you an officer or committeeman?	No. of mtgs. held per year	No. of mtgs. resp't. attends

3. Does your wife belong to any voluntary organizations?

Name	Is she an officer or committeeman?	No. of mtgs. held per year	How often does she attend?
_____	_____	_____	_____
_____	_____	_____	_____
_____	_____	_____	_____
_____	_____	_____	_____
_____	_____	_____	_____
_____	_____	_____	_____
_____	_____	_____	_____
_____	_____	_____	_____

4. Now I would like to read off some situations we all face in our daily lives. Would you tell me what proportion of contact you have with whites in these situations?

	in your home	at work	at parties	in vol. orgs.	when you were in school	where you grew up
none	____	____	____	____	____	____
once a month or less	____	____	____	____	____	____
once a week	____	____	____	____	____	____
every day	____	____	____	____	____	____

5. Is this enough contact or would you like more? In what areas? Why?

5a. *FOR OLDER RESPONDENTS ONLY. Do you have more or less contact now than you did when you were about thirty?

                More_____   Less_____

6. Do you now participate or have you ever participated in any way in civil rights?

IF YES a. What groups?

          b. What was your specific action in this group(s)?

          c. Do you participate less, as much, or more than before?

               In what way?   Why?

7. Some people who lived a large portion of their lives before the civil rights movement vented their feelings toward inequality in a less organized way, such as taking white and colored signs off of buildings and throwing them away. Have you ever done anything along these lines of unorganized protest?

8. Now I would like to find out something about your interest in the mass media. What newspapers do you read regularly?

Name	Frequency	What do you most enjoy about this paper?

Do you happen to read the *Chicago Defender?* Yes_____ No_____

9. Do you happen to read any magazines regularly?

Name	Frequency	What do you like most about this magazine?

10. Do you listen to the radio much?

Station	What types of programs?	About how many hours per week?

11. W-4 What are your favorite TV programs — the ones you almost always watch?

_____   _____

_____   _____

_____   _____

_____   _____

12. What is your favorite type of program?

13. W-6 How many hours have you usually watched TV on recent Saturdays?

Average_____

14. W-7 How about Sundays? What would you say is the average number of hours you've watched TV on recent Sundays?

_____

15. Adding them all up now, how many hours per week do you watch TV?

_____Average week.

16. Now I am going to hand you a sheet which contains a list of different troubles or complaints people sometimes have. GIVE RESPONDENT PAGE B. (See p. 163). For each one please check off how often you were bothered by such a complaint during the last week.

17. Now I am going to read you a list of statements. Would you give me your opinion in the terms listed on this card? GIVE RESPONDENT CARD A (See p. 164).

18. c+1   a It's better to go along with the crowd than to be a martyr.   _____

    f+1   b Any good leader must be tough with the people he leads so as to gain their respect.   _____

    a0−1   c Like every other group, I believe that there are both good and bad whites in this country.   _____

    c+2   d When almost everyone agrees on something, there is little reason to oppose it.   _____

f−1	e	People tend to put too much importance on respect for authority.	_____
ao+1	f	The trouble with most people is that they think they are better than other people.	_____
c−3	g	I like to fool around with new ideas, even if they turn out later to be a total waste of time.	_____
f+2	h	People can be divided into two classes — the weak and the strong.	_____
ao−2	i	Most white people are not prejudiced and sincerely believe that Negroes are equals.	_____
c−4	j	Some of my best friends think that my ideas are impractical, if not a bit wild.	_____
f−2	k	Sometimes it is best to discourage complete obedience to orders.	_____
m+2	l	No oppressed group has ever gotten justice except by its own blood, sweat, and tears.	_____
c−5	m	There is no reason why close friends should have similar opinions about things.	_____
f+3	n	No sane, normal, or decent person could ever think of hurting a close friend or relative.	_____
a1−2	o	It makes me mad to see how little pride Negroes take in their own group.	_____
c−6	p	I prefer games in which one individual competes against another rather than team games.	_____
f−3	q	I seldom have any enthusiasm about respecting and obeying authorities.	_____
a1+3	r	White people should make more of a distinction between respectable Negroes and non-respectable Negroes.	_____
f+4	s	Obedience and respect for authority are absolutely the most important virtues children should learn.	_____
ac+3	t	It is risky to trust a white person.	_____

a1 − 3   u   I think too many Negroes want to be white — rather than taking a prominent part in their own race's affairs.   _____

ac − 4   v   Jews have never endured the sorts of discrimination that Negroes have faced.   _____

c + 9   w   It is best not to express your views when in the company of friends who disagree with you.   _____

ao + 2   x   Many white people are only friendly to Negroes when they want something out of them.   _____

c + 10   y   Before a person does something, he should try to consider how his friends will react to it.   _____

f − 5   z   People would do well to try to retain some of the rebelliousness of youth in their later years.   _____

19. m − 1 a   A man gets ahead better by keeping out of trouble rather than always demanding his rights.   _____

sv + 1   b   I sometimes feel that prejudice in this country has hurt me personally.   _____

c − 7   c   Sometimes I rather enjoy going against the rules and doing things I'm not supposed to.   _____

a1 + 1   d   If all Negroes behaved themselves properly, no Negroes would run into prejudice.   _____

m + 1   e   Negroes don't fight hard enough for their rights. _____

f − 4   f   It may well be that children who talk back to their parents actually end up later respecting them more.

                                                                            _____

a1 − 1   g   Too many Negroes try to remain aloof and avoid activities within their own race.   _____

m − 2   h   If Negroes push too hard for equal rights they may lose the gains they've made so far.   _____

a1 + 2   i   Negro-Americans bring on themselves much of the discrimination they face — by not working hard enough in school and on the job.   _____

sv − 4   j   Even if there were no racial prejudices and discrimination in America, I don't think my life would be any different.   _____

m − 3   k   Before pushing for more rights, Negro-Americans need to work first on improving their own neighborhoods.   _____

sv − 3   l   I really cannot say that prejudice and discrimination have ever seriously affected my life.   _____

ac + 4   m   It is simply not true that Jews are too rich and too powerful in this country.   _____

sv + 2   n   There have been times when I couldn't get something I wanted because of group discrimination.   _____

ac + 5   o   Negroes can expect no real help from most white people in this fight against racial discrimination. _____

m + 3   p   In seeking to end racial discrimination, Negro-Americans need to stop talking so much and to start more economic boycotts and other direct action.

_____

ac − 3   q   Young people should be allowed to marry whomever they want regardless of religion or race.   _____

TAKE CARD A BACK.

20.   How do you feel about Negroes who try to "pass"?

21.   Do you feel that the fact that Negroes originally came from Africa is an advantage or a disadvantage?   Why?

22.   What are your feelings toward interracial marriage?

23.   What is your opinion of the middle-class, white-collar Negro in the United States? Probe. . . . . .

24.   What is your opinion of the lower-class Negro in the United States?

25.   Do you think that lower-class Negroes can rise up from the ghettos that they live in and make a better life for themselves? Yes_____ No_____

Why, or why not?

26.   Would you rather work for a company run by a Negro or a white man — or wouldn't it make much difference to you?

White_____   Negro_____   No difference_____

PROBE INCOME

27. If you had your choice would you rather work alongside:

All Negroes _____
Mostly Negroes _____
Half and half _____
Mostly whites _____
All whites _____
No difference _____

Why?

28. If you had your choice of neighborhoods to live in, would you rather live with:

All Negroes _____
Mostly Negroes _____
Half and half _____
Mostly whites _____
No difference _____

Why?

29. Do you feel that there are basic differences between the races as groups of people?

Yes _____   No _____

If YES, what are they?

30. Do you think that you would ever find it a little distasteful to:

Age 30

Eat at the same table with a white   _____ _____
Dance with a white   _____ _____
Go to a party and find that most
of the people there were white   _____ _____
Have a white marry someone in
your family   _____ _____

31. *ONLY FOR OLDER RESPONDENTS. How did you feel about these things at age 30? RECORD ABOVE.

32. How did your parents (guardian) feel about these things?

33. Do you think that you would ever find it a little distasteful to:

Eat at the same table with a Jew   _____
Dance with a Jew   _____
Go to a party and find that most
  of the people there were Jews   _____
Have a Jew marry someone in your
  family   _____

34. Many people of our race feel hostility toward the white man. In other words they feel anger toward a particular white or whites in general.

a. Do you ever feel anger or hostility toward a white man or whites in general? Probe.

b. Under what circumstances has this happened? GET DETAIL

c. What did you do during or after the situation to relieve this anger or hostility? Probe.

*FOR OLDER RESPONDENTS ONLY. Do you feel that you are more or less hostile toward whites than when you were about 30 years old?

            More_____   Less_____

35. In your opinion, do you feel that the recent gains made in civil rights were due in part to the increased awareness of northern whites to the plight of the Negro?

36. Many people of our race have experienced specific instances of discrimination as well as being aware that they are discriminated against generally.
Would you say that you have experienced:

Very little   _____
Some   _____
A great deal   _____ of discrimination?

Would you tell me about some of these experiences and the age at which they happened?

Age_____   Experience   Would you say that it affected you
                             very little, quite a bit, or a
                             great deal?

37. Thinking back now over your experiences, would you say that taken all together, they have had much of an effect on your life? Yes_____ No_____

If YES, in what way?

38. If you were asked to use one of these four names for your social class, which would you say you belonged in: The middle class_____, the lower class_____, the working class_____, or the upper class_____?

39. Do you own an automobile? More than one? What is the year and make of your automobile(s)?

40. Some people put a lot of emphasis on clothing and dress and others don't pay much attention to it. What are your feelings about the importance of dress?

41. We would like to get some idea of what people do in their leisure time. What are some of the things you do for recreation and how often do you do them?

Item	Frequency	Who do you do this with?
_____	_____	_____
_____	_____	_____
_____	_____	_____
_____	_____	_____

42. *FOR OLDER RESPONDENTS ONLY. Have you changed your leisure time activities since you were about thirty? In what way?

43. Do you happen to remember what your parents did in their leisure time? What were some of the things they did as you remember?

44. What do you usually do on your vacation?

45. Do you engage in many of the so-called cultural activities? I am going to read you a list of these. Would you tell me if you engage in them and how often?

Attend classical musical concerts _____
Attend plays _____
Attend folk music concerts _____
Attend jazz concerts _____
Play a musical instrument _____
Read books. . . .of what type _____
Attend public lectures _____
Visit museums or art galleries _____

46. Do you ever take a drink (beer, whiskey, or any other alcoholic drink)?

Yes_____   No_____

If YES: Did you take a drink last week? Yes_____ No_____

About how many times did you take a drink during the past week?

Once or twice _____
3-4 times _____
Nearly every day _____
Once a day _____
Two or more times a day _____

Is that more or less than usual? More_____ Less_____ Same_____

During the past week was there any time, times, when you got high (got so you were feeling no pain)? Yes_____ No_____

How often do you drink alcoholic beverages at:

Your home
Friends' homes
Restaurants, bars, clubs

47. *FOR OLDER RESPONDENTS ONLY. Do you drink more_____ or less_____ now than you did at age 30?

48. Which of the following do you buy on credit?

House _____
Auto _____
TV _____
Clothes _____
Food _____

49. How do you feel about credit buying? Probe. . . . . . .

50. Do you attempt to save? Yes_____ No_____
     If YES: How successful are you?

                         Very successful   _____
                         Somewhat successful   _____
                         Unsuccessful   _____

51. Do you now or did you ever belong to a high school or college
     fraternity?

                                                        Are you still
        Name   High school   College   active?

        _____   _____   _____   _____

        _____   _____   _____   _____

52. What do you consider your political party affiliation?

                         Democrat   _____
                         Republican   _____
                         Independent   _____
                         Other   _____

53. Did you vote in the 1964 election? Yes_____ No_____

54. Could you tell me if you voted straight party or split ticket?

        Straight ticket   Dem._____
                             Rep._____

        Split ticket mostly Dem._____
                             Rep._____

        Other (specify)   _____

55. Generally speaking, would you say that you personally care a good
     deal which party wins the presidential elections?

                         Care very much   _____
                         Care   _____
                         Pro-con it depends _____

Don't care much   _____
Don't care at all   _____

56. Some people don't pay much attention to the political campaigns.
How about you, would you say that you have been very much interested, somewhat interested or not much interested in the campaigns
of 1964?

Very much interested _____
Somewhat interested _____
Not much interested _____

57. What is your opinion of the Daley Democratic machine in Chicago?

58. What is your opinion of Congressman Dawson?

58a. IF RESPONDENT INDICATES HOSTILITY TO DAWSON,
ASK:
Have you participated in any of the efforts to run independent
candidates in Chicago? IF YES: How?

59. How do you feel about Superintendent Willis?

60. What is this address?

61. INTERVIEWER ASSESS SKIN SHADE

	Male	Female (if possible)
Dark Brown	_____	_____
Brown	_____	_____
Fair	_____	_____
"Passable"	_____	_____

62. How long have you lived at this address?

63. How long have you lived in Chicago?

64. In what year were you born?

65. Where were you born? GET SPECIFIC PLACE

66. Where were you raised? By whom? IF NOT PARENTS, FIND OUT WHY.

67. What is your marital status? If married, is this your first marriage? If not, what were the dates and reasons for the terminations of earlier marriages?

68. Could you tell me where your wife was born?

69. Could you tell me in what year your wife was born?

70. Where was she raised and by whom? IF NOT PARENTS, FIND OUT WHY.

71. Who lives at this address with you? RECORD RESPONDENT HERE ALSO

Relationship	Age	If school age children, record name of school here
_____	____	_____
_____	____	_____
_____	____	_____
_____	____	_____
_____	____	_____
_____	____	_____

72. Do you have any sons and/or daughters who do not live at this address?

Relationship	Age	Address	Occupation IF COLLEGE GET NAME, GET OCC. OF HUSBAND OR MARRIED DAUGHTERS
_____	____	_____	_____
_____	____	_____	_____
_____	____	_____	_____
_____	____	_____	_____
_____	____	_____	_____

73. Where and how much education have you attained?

Grades	School name	Location	Years attended	Grad-uated
_____	_____	_____	_____	_____
_____	_____	_____	_____	_____
_____	_____	_____	_____	_____
_____	_____	_____	_____	_____
_____	_____	_____	_____	_____
_____	_____	_____	_____	_____

IF COLLEGE: What did you major in in college?

74. Could you tell me how much education your wife has received?

75. Where did you first meet your wife?

76. What is your present occupation? GET FIRM NAME AND SPE-CIFIC OCCUPATION.

77. You said you are a (SPECIFY MAIN JOB). How many hours a week do you usually work at this job?   _____hours.

78. What time do you usually start and stop work on a regular weekday? Start_____ Stop_____

79. How many evenings a week do you do any work? _____None _____Evenings

80. Counting both Saturdays and Sundays, about how many hours do you generally put in on a weekend? _____None _____Hours

81. What was the first full-time job that you took?

82. What was your father's or guardian's occupation?

83. How much education did he receive?

84. What was your mother's occupation?

85. How much education did she receive?

86. Does your wife work? What is her occupation?

87. Could you tell me her father's occupation?

88. Could you tell me her mother's occupation?

89. Would you look at this card and please tell me the letter which approximates *your* yearly income from your job? GIVE RESPONDENT CARD B.

90. Would you give me the letter which approximates your wife's income?

91. Do you have any other source of income other than yours and your wife's? From what source? Would you tell me the letter on the card which approximates your yearly income from this source?

92. Do you have any religious preference? IF YES: What is that?

93. IF YES, has this always been your preference?

    IF NOT: What was it before?

    What made you change?

94. IF YES: Do you attend any specific church? What is the name of it?

    How often do you usually attend?

95. Compared to most (SPECIFIC DENOMINATIONAL REFERENCE) do you consider your religious identification to be:

    Strong_____ Moderate_____ Weak_____

96. Does your wife have a religious preference? IF YES: What is that?

97. IF YES: Does your wife attend a specific church? What is the name of it?

    IF YES: How often does she usually attend?

98. Would you tell me how many brothers and sisters you grew up with?

99. Would you like to have any more children? How many?

Interviewer Data Evaluation Form — to be completed immediately after leaving respondent's house

1. What is the age of respondent's house____apartment____?
    Old (pre-World War I)____ Intermediate (between Wars)____
    New (since World War II)____

2. What is the size of respondent's home?

    Large (8 or more rooms)____ Medium (4-7 rooms)____ Small (under 4 rooms)____

3. Are the houses in R's block closely spaced or what?

    Closely spaced____ Widely spaced____

4. Does the size of R's house differ from the others in the block?

    Yes____ No____; if yes, how?____

5. Is the exterior of R's house kept up nicely, average, or run down?

    Kept up____ Average____ Run down____

6. Does R's house differ externally from the other houses in the block?

    No____ Yes____; if yes, how____

7. General description of R's living room furniture (e.g., modern, traditional, over-stuffed, expensive, cheap, good condition, worn).

    _____

    _____

8. Over-all rating of level of living: Excellent_____ Above aver-
   age_____ Average_____ Below average_____ Poor_____

9. Is that interview of questionable value, generally adequate, or high
   quality?

   Questionable_____ Adequate_____ High quality_____
   If questionable, why?_____

   _____

10. How was rapport with respondent? Excellent_____ Average_____
    Poor_____

11. What was R's interest in the interview? High_____ Average_____
    Low_____

12. What was the interview setting? _____

    _____

13. Who else was present during the interview and what effect did this
    have?

    Persons present   How long   What effect

    _____   _____   _____

    _____   _____   _____

    _____   _____   _____

PAGE A

		1	2	3	4
a	To have plenty of time for leisure activities				
b	To be helpful to others				
c	To have a close family relationship				
d	To have good, close friends				

		1	2	3	4
e	To have enough money to live well				
f	To be active in community organizations				
g	To attend concerts, plays, and other artistic and cultural events				
h	To have a nice, well-furnished house				
i	To have freedom from pressures to conform				
j	To live in a good neighborhood for my children to grow up in				
k	To do something important				
l	To be original and creative				
m	To have recognition in my career				
n	To contribute to national or international betterment				
o	Other (write in)				
	Which of the above do you consider the most important?				

PAGE B

Symptoms		Not at all	One or two times	Several times	Nearly all week
a	Back pains				
b	Cold sweats				

Symptoms		Not at all	One or two times	Several times	Nearly all week
c	Common cold	_____	_____	_____	_____
d	Constipation	_____	_____	_____	_____
e	Diarrhea	_____	_____	_____	_____
f	Dizziness	_____	_____	_____	_____
g	Fever	_____	_____	_____	_____
h	General aches and pains	_____	_____	_____	_____
i	Headaches	_____	_____	_____	_____
j	Loss of appetite	_____	_____	_____	_____
k	Muscle twitches or trembling	_____	_____	_____	_____
l	Nervousness or tensions	_____	_____	_____	_____
m	Rapid heart beat	_____	_____	_____	_____
n	Skin rashes	_____	_____	_____	_____
o	Upset stomach	_____	_____	_____	_____

CARD A

1	Strongly agree
2	Agree
3	It depends, not sure
4	Disagree
5	Strongly disagree

Appendix B

Indexes

Seven indexes were constructed from questions nineteen and twenty in the questionnaire. These items were taken from a study of middle-income black families in Boston (Freeman 1965) and included the following:

> Anti-white attitudes
> Anti-black attitudes
> Militancy
> Authoritarianism
> Anti-Semitism
> Subjective victimization
> Conformity

Indexes were constructed in the following manner. Each statement was determined as either positive or negative. If the respondent answered either Strongly Agree or Agree to a positive statement, he was given a score of three (3). If he answered Pro-Con or It Depends, he was given a score of two (2); and if he answered Disagree or Strongly Disagree, he was given a score of one (1). This procedure was reversed for negative items. Therefore, the higher the score for an individual, the higher his disposition on a particular index. For example, a person who scored a twenty-four (24) on the authoritarian index would be more authoritarian than the person who scored twelve (12). After all eighty respondents were scored in this manner, the mean was obtained and each person was classified as either "High or "Low" on each index depending on whether he fell above or below the mean. In this manner the white-collar sample was dichotomized for each index. The same procedure was used for the blue-collar sample. On the following pages are the indexes and their characteristics.

ANTI-WHITE INDEX

Positive

Negroes can expect no real help from most white people in this fight against racial discrimination.

It is risky to trust a white person.

Many white people are only friendly to Negroes when they want something out of them.

The trouble with most white people is that they think they are better than other people.

Negative

Like every other group, I believe that there are both good and bad whites in this country.

Most white people are not prejudiced and sincerely believe that Negroes are equals.

Young people should be allowed to marry whomever they want regardless of religion or race.

	White-Collar (N = 60)	Blue-Collar (N = 20)
Mean	12.3	13.8
Range	7-20	9-21

ANTI-BLACK INDEX

Positive

White people should make more of a distinction between respectable Negroes who are like them and the poorly educated Negroes who are a group of their own.

Negro Americans bring on themselves much of the discrimination they face — by not working hard enough in school and on the job.

If all Negroes behaved themselves properly, no Negroes would run into prejudice.

Negative

Too many Negroes try to remain aloof and avoid activities within their own race.

It makes me mad to see how little pride many Negroes take in their own group.

I think too many Negroes want to be white — rather than taking a prominent part in their own race's affairs.

	White-Collar (N=60)	Blue-Collar (N=20)
Mean	10.2	11.1
Range	6-16	9-14

MILITANCY INDEX

Positive

In seeking to end racial discrimination, Negro-Americans need to stop talking so much and to start more economic boycotts and other direct actions.

No oppressed group has ever gotten justice except by its own blood, sweat, and tears.

Negroes, don't fight hard enough for their rights.

Negative

A man gets ahead better by keeping out of trouble rather than always demanding his rights.

If Negroes push too hard for equal rights they may lose the gains they've made so far.

Before pushing for more rights, Negro-Americans need to work first on improving their own neighborhoods.

	White-Collar (N=60)	Blue-Collar (N=20)
Mean	14.9	15.2
Range	10-18	10-18

AUTHORITARIANISM INDEX

Positive

Obedience and respect for authority are absolutely the most important virtues children should learn.

No sane, normal, or decent person could ever think of hurting a close friend or relative.

People can be divided into two classes — the weak and the strong.

Any good leader must be tough with the people he heads so as to gain their respect.

Negative

People tend to put too much importance on respect for authority.

Sometimes it is best to discourage complete obedience to orders.

I seldom have any enthusiasm about respecting and obeying authorities.

It may well be that children who talk back to their parents actually end up later respecting them more.

People would do well to try to retain some of the rebelliousness of youth in their later years.

	White-Collar ($N=60$)	Blue-Collar ($N=20$)
Mean	17.9	21.4
Range	11-26	17-25

CONFORMITY INDEX

Positive

Before a person does something, he should try to consider how his friends will react to it.

It is best not to express your views when in the company of friends who disagree with you.

When almost everyone agrees on something, there is little reason to oppose it.

It's better to go along with the crowd than to be a martyr.

Negative

I like to fool around with new ideas, even if they turn out later to be a total waste of time.

Some of my best friends think that my ideas are impractical, if not a bit wild.

There is no reason why close friends should have similar opinions about things.

I prefer games in which one individual competes against another rather than team games.

Sometimes I rather enjoy going against the rules and doing things I'm not supposed to.

	White-Collar (N = 60)	Blue-Collar (N = 20)
Mean	14.6	16.8
Range	10-21	12-22

SUBJECTIVE VICTIMIZATION INDEX[1]

Positive

There have been times when I couldn't get something I wanted because of group discrimination.

I sometimes feel that prejudice in this country has hurt me personally.

Negative

Even if there were no racial prejudice and discrimination in America I don't think my life would be any different.

---

[1]This item was not used for analysis because over three-fourths of each group scored the maximum, indicating that the item did not discriminate and there was almost no variance to explain.

I really cannot say that prejudice and discrimination have ever seriously affected my life.

	White-Collar (N = 60)	Blue-Collar (N = 20)
Mean	11.8	11.8
Range	6-12	6-12

ANTI-SEMITISM INDEX

It is simply not true that Jews are too rich and powerful in this country.

	White-Collar (N = 60)	Blue-Collar (N = 20)
Agree or Strongly Agree (Low Anti-Semitic)	53%	40%
Strongly Disagree, Disagree, or It Depends (High Anti-Semitic	47%	60%

INTERRELATIONSHIPS OF INDEXES

The interrelationships of these indexes, except for the Subjective Victimization index which was omitted, was obtained by cross-tabulating one by the other after dichotomization. The following two tables give the Q values, Chi-Square values, and significances of these interrelationships for the middle-class, white-collar sample.

Q Association of Indexes

	Anti-White	Anti-Negro	Militancy	Authoritarianism	Conformity	Anti-Semitism
Anti-White	. .	+.02	+.38	+.06	—.46	—.22
Anti-Black		. .	—.56	+.08	+.06	—.33
Militancy			. .	—.69	+.10	—.14
Authoritarianism				. .	+.38	+.49
Conformity					. .	+.10
Anti-Semitism						. .

CHI-SQUARE VALUES AND SIGNIFICANCE LEVELS
OF THE SIGNIFICANT INTERRELATIONS
BETWEEN THE INDEXES

	A-W	A-N	Mil.	F	C	A-S
A-W	. .	n.s.	n.s.	n.s.	n.s.	n.s.
A-N		. .	$X^2=5.7$ p.=.05	n.s.	n.s.	n.s.
Mil.			. .	$X^2=9.6$ p.=.01	n.s.	n.s.
F.				. .	n.s.	$X^2=4.2$ p.=.05
C.					. .	n.s.
A-S						. .

Bibliography

ALLPORT, GORDON W. *The Nature of Prejudice.* Garden City: Doubleday, 1958.

_____ . *The Use of Personal Documents in Psychological Sciences.* New York: Social Science Research Council, 1942.

BACK, KURT W., and SIMPSON, IDA HARPER. "The Dilemma of the Negro Professional." *The Journal of Social Issues* 20, no. 2 (April 1964): 60-70.

BAIN, READ. "The Validity of Life Histories and Diaries." *Journal of Educational Research* 3 (1929): 156-61.

BANKS, W. S. M. "The Rank Order of Sensitivity to Discriminations of Negroes in Columbus, Ohio." *American Sociological Review* 15, no. 4 (August 1950): 529-34.

BAUER, RAYMOND et al. "The Marketing Dilemma of Negroes." *Journal of Marketing* 29 (1965): 1-6.

BLUMER, HERBERT. *An Appraisal of Thomas and Znaniecki's The Polish Peasant in Europe and America: Critique of Research in the Social Sciences: 1.* New York: Social Science Research Council, 1939.

BRINK, WILLIAM, and HARRIS, LOUIS. *The Negro Revolution in America.* New York: Simon and Schuster, 1964.

BROOM, LEONARD, and GLENN, NORVAL D. *Transformation of the Negro American.* New York: Harper and Row, 1965.

CALIVER, AMBROSE. *A Background Study of Negro College Students.* Washington, D.C.: Government Printing Office, 1933.

CAPLOVITZ, DAVID. *The Poor Pay More.* New York: The Free Press of of Glencoe, 1963.

CRUSE, HAROLD. *The Crisis of the Negro Intellectual.* New York: William Morrow, 1967.

CURTAIN, PHILIP D. "Africa and the Beginning." In *Black History,* edited by Melvin Drimmer. Garden City: Doubleday, 1968, pp. 12-33.

DAVIS, ALLISON W.; GARDNER, BURLEIGH B.; and GARDNER, MARY R. *Deep South.* Chicago: The University of Chicago Press, 1941.

DOLLARD, JOHN. *Criteria for the Life History.* New Haven, Conn.: Yale University Press, 1935.

_____.*Caste and Class in a Southern Town.* Garden City: Doubleday, 1957.

DRAKE, ST. CLAIR, and CAYTON, HORACE. *Black Metropolis.* New York and Evanston: Harper and Row, 1962.

DUBOIS, CORA. *The People of Alor.* Cambridge, Mass.: Harvard University Press, 1960.

DUBOIS, W. E. BURGHARDT. "The Talented Tenth." In *The Negro Problem,* edited by Booker T. Washington et al. New York: James Pott & Co., 1903, pp. 33-75.

DURKHEIM, EMILE. *Le Suicide: Etude De Sociologie.* Paris: F. Alcan, 1897. In English. *Suicide: A Study in Sociology.* New York: The Free Press of Glencoe, 1951.

EISENSTADT, S. N. "Social Change, Differentiation, and Evolution." *American Sociological Review* 24, no. 3 (June 1, 1964): 375-85.

Employment and Earnings. Bureau of Labor Statistics, vol. 16, no. 11, May 1970.

ESSIEN-UDOM, E. U. *Black Nationalism: A Search for an Identity in America.* New York: Dell Publishing Company, 1962.

FRANKLIN, JOHN HOPE. "The Two Worlds of Race: A Historical View." *Daedalus* 94, no. 4 (Fall 1965): 899-920.

FRAZIER, E. FRANKLIN. *The Negro Family in the United States.* Chicago: The University of Chicago Press, 1967.

_____. *Black Bourgeoisie.* New York: Collier Books, 1962.

FREEMAN, HOWARD E. et al. "Color, Class, and Attitudes Among Middle Income Negroes." Unpublished paper by the Florence Heller Graduate School for Advanced Studies in Social Welfare, Brandeis University, Boston, 1965.

GINZBERG, ELI et al. *The Middle Class Negro in the White Man's World.* New York: Columbia University Press, 1967.

GLENN, NORVAL D. "Negro Prestige Criteria: A Case Study in the Bases of Prestige." *American Journal of Sociology* 68, May 1963.

HARE, NATHAN. "The Changing Occupational Status of the Negro in the United States: An Intracohort Analysis." Unpublished Ph.D. dissertation, University of Chicago, 1962.

_____. *The Black Anglo-Saxons.* New York: Marzani and Munsell, Inc., 1965.

HARTMANN, HEINZ. "The Mutual Influences on the Development of the Ego and Id." *The Psychoanalytic Study of the Child* 7 (1952): 9-30.

_____. "Comments on the Psychoanalytic Theory of the Ego." *The Psychoanalytic Study of the Child* 5 (1950): 74-96.

HOMANS, GEORGE C. *Social Behavior: Its Elementary Forms.* New York: Harcourt, Brace and World, 1961.

HORNEY, KAREN. *Our Inner Conflicts.* New York: W. W. Norton and Co., 1945.

HUGHES, HELEN MAGGILL, and WATTS, LEWIS G. "Portrait of the Self-Integrator." *The Journal of Social Issues* 20, no. 2 (April 1964): 193-15.

JACOBSON, P. H. *American Marriage and Divorce.* New York: Rinehart, 1959.

JANOWITZ, MORRIS, and BETTLEHEIM, BRUNO. *Social Change and Prejudice.* New York: The Free Press of Glencoe, 1964.

JOHNSON, CHARLES S. *Patterns of Negro Segregation.* New York: Harper and Brothers, 1943.

KARDINER, ABRAM, and OVESEY, LIONEL. *The Mark of Oppression.* New York: W. W. Norton and Co., 1951.

KARON, B. P. *The Negro Personality.* New York: Springer, 1958.

KILLIAN, LEWIS M. *The Impossible Revolution? Black Power and the American Dream.* New York: Random House, 1968.

KILLINGSWORTH, CHARLES C. "Jobs and Income for Negroes." In *Race and the Social Sciences,* edited by Irwin Katz and Patricia Gunn. New York: Basic Books, 1969, pp. 194-273.

LASSWELL, HAROLD D. *Politics: Who Gets What, When, How.* Cleveland: The World Publishing Company, 1936.

LEWIS, HYLAN. "Social Differentiation in the Negro Community." Unpublished Ph.D. dissertation, University of Chicago, 1936.

LINCOLN, C. ERIC. *The Black Muslims in America.* Boston: Beacon Press, 1961.

MARX, GARY T. *Protest and Prejudice: A Study of Belief in the Black Community.* New York: Harper and Row, 1967.

MCCORD, WILLIAM; HOWARD, JOHN; FRIEDBERG, BERNARD; and HARWOOD, EDWIN. *Life Styles in the Black Ghetto.* New York: W. W. Norton and Co., 1969.

MERTON, ROBERT K. *Social Theory and Social Structure.* rev. ed. New York: The Free Press, 1957.

MOORE, WILLIAM R., JR. *The Vertical Ghetto: Everyday Life in an Urban Project.* New York: Random House, 1969.

MOYNIHAN, DANIEL PATRICK. "Employment, Income and the Ordeal of the Negro Family." *Daedalus* 94, no. 4 (Fall 1965): 745-70.

MYRDAL, GUNNAR. *An American Dilemma.* New York: McGraw-Hill, 1964.

NOEL, DONALD L. "Group Identification Among Negroes: An Empirical Analysis." *The Journal of Social Issues* 20 (April 1964): 71-84.

OSSOWSKI, STANISLAW. "Different Conceptions of Social Class." In *Class, Status, and Power,* edited by Reinhard Bendix and Seymour Martin Lipset. New York: The Free Press, 1966, pp. 86-96.

PARKER, SEYMOUR, and KLEINER, ROBERT J. *Mental Illness in the Urban Negro Community.* New York: The Free Press, 1966.

PETTIGREW, THOMAS F. *A Profile of the Negro American.* Princeton, N. J.: D. Van Nostrand, 1964.

PINKNEY, ALPHONSO. *Black Americans.* Englewood Cliffs, N. J.; Prentice-Hall, Inc., 1969.

REUTER, EDWARD BYRON. *The Mulatto in the United States.* Boston: R. G. Badger, 1918.

ROHRER, JOHN H. et al. *The Eighth Generation.* New York: Harper and Brothers, 1960.

ROSE, ARNOLD. *The Negro's Morale.* Minneapolis: The University of Minnesota Press, 1949.

ROSENZWEIG, S. "The Picture-Association Method and its Application in a Study to Reactions to Frustration." *Journal of Personality*, no. 14, (1945), pp. 3-23.

SIMPSON, RICHARD L. "Negro-Jewish Prejudice Authoritarianism and Some Social Variables as Correlates." *Social Problems*, no. 7 (March 1959), pp. 138-46.

SKOLNICK, JEROME. *The Politics of Protest.* New York: Simon and Schuster, 1969.

STAFFORD, JAMES E.; COX, KEITH K.; and HIGGINBOTHAM, JAMES B. "Some Consumption Pattern Differences Between Urban Whites and Negroes." In *Blacks in the United States*, edited by Norval D. Glenn and Charles M. Bonjean. San Francisco: Chandler, 1968, pp. 87-98.

STEIN, ROBERT L., and TRAVIS, HERMAN. "Labor Force Employment in 1960." *Labor Force Reports*, no. 14 (April 1961), pp. A-25, Table C-7.

STOUFFER, SAMUEL A. *Communism, Conformity, and Civil Liberties.* Garden City: Doubleday, 1955.

STRONG, SAMUEL. "Social Types in the Negro Community of Chicago." Unpublished Ph.D. dissertation, University of Chicago, 1962.

————. "The Negro Market, Accent on Quality." *Media-scope.* April 1964, p. 77.

The Social and Economic Status of Negroes in the United States, 1969. BLS Report no. 375, *Current Population Reports*, Series P-23, no. 29, 1967.

U.S. BUREAU OF THE CENSUS. *Statistical Abstract of the United States.* National Data Book and Guide to Sources, 90th edition, 1969.

U.S. DEPARTMENT OF COMMERCE, BUREAU OF THE CENSUS. *Current Population Reports.* Series P-60, no. 66, December 23, 1969.

U.S. DEPARTMENT OF COMMERCE, BUSINESS, AND DEFENSE SERVICES ADMISTRATION. *A Guide to Negro Marketing Information.* Washington, D.C.: Government Printing Office, 1966.

WATTS, LEWIS G. et al. *The Middle-Income Negro Family Faces Urban Renewal.* A Report to the Department of Commerce and Development, Commonwealth of Massachusetts, 1964. Prepared by the Research Center of the Florence Heller Graduate School for Advanced Studies in Social Welfare, Brandeis University, Boston.

WEBER, MAX. *Essays in Sociology.* Translated with an introduction by Hans H. Gerth and C. Wright Mills. New York: Oxford University Press, 1958.

WESTIE, FRANK R., and HOWARD, DONALD H. "Social Status Differentials and the Race Attitudes of Negroes." *American Sociological Review* 19 (October 1954): 584-90.

WILENSKY, HAROLD L., and LEBEAUX, CHARLES. *Industrial Society and Social Welfare.* New York: The Free Press of Glencoe, 1965.

WILLIAMS, ROBIN M., JR. *Strangers Next Door: Ethnic Relations in American Communities.* Englewood Cliffs, N. J.: Prentice-Hall, Inc., 1964.

WILSON, JAMES Q. *Negro Politics: The Search For Leadership.* New York: The Free Press, 1960.

WOODSON, CARTER GOODWIN. *The Negro Professional Man and the Community.* Washington, D.C.: The Association for the Study of Negro Life and History, Inc., 1934.

YOUNG, PAULINE V. *Scientific Social Surveys and Research.* Englewood Cliffs, N. J.: Prentice-Hall, Inc., 1966.

Index

Black middle class (*continued*)
21, 23-25, 27, 28, 41, 73, 74,
129, 130, 137, 139, 140, 142;
marriage in, 9, 10, 22, 23, 45,
72, 75, 85, 129; occupational
attainment of, 6, 7, 8, 9, 15, 19,
20, 23, 28, 38, 68, 69, 70, 71,
130; political position of, 14, 21,
28, 29, 36, 37, 38, 49, 51, 130,
141, 142; social phychology of,
11, 16, 21, 138-39, 141
Black militancy, 15, 35, 53-54, 67,
78, 79, 105, 128, 130, 137, 138,
141, 142
Black Muslims. *See* Religion, Muslim
Black Nationalist groups, 54, 65.
See also Religion, Muslim
Blue-collar workers. *See* Black labor
force, blue-collar workers

Cayton, Horace, 9, 23, 39, 41,
42, 134
Chatham community, 16, 23, 29,
132
Civil rights activities, 9, 12, 15, 20,
33, 35-36, 39, 51, 53-54, 65, 67,
74, 75-76, 80, 81, 85, 91, 92, 99,
103, 105, 128, 130, 132, 134,
135, 138, 139, 141, 142, 143
Conformity, 60, 61, 63, 68
Consumption patterns, 25-26,
47-48
Craftsmen. *See* Artisans

Daley machine, 38, 49-51, 94
Dawson, William, 37-38, 49-50, 94
Democratic party, 36-37, 39,
48-49, 142
Demographic changes, 20, 21, 68,
70, 71, 131, 142
Desegregation, 1-2, 28. *See also*
Interracial contact
Discrimination, 12, 35, 56-57,
65-66, 67, 76, 78-79, 86, 98, 99,
104, 128, 131, 137, 138.
See also Segregation

Dollard, John, 2, 9
Drake, St. Clair, 9, 23, 39, 41, 42,
134
DuBois, W. E. B., 1, 5

Education. *See* Black middle class;
Socioeconomic status
Ego defenses, 13, 19, 20, 27, 28,
64, 66, 67, 70, 71, 72-74, 75,
76, 80, 86, 92, 103-4, 105,
131, 139

Field hands, 3
Fraternal organizations, 74, 75,
76, 134
Frazier, E. Franklin, 9, 11, 13-14,
15, 19, 20-21, 22-23, 24, 27, 34,
39, 41, 42, 52, 70, 74, 78, 134,
136, 138-39
Free Negroes, 3

Hare, Nathan, 13-14, 23, 27, 42
Horney, Karen, 66, 139
Hostility. *See* Interracial attitudes;
Intraracial attitudes
Household servants, 3-4, 19

Income. *See* Black middle class;
Socioeconomic status
Inferiority feelings, 11, 12, 19, 27,
28, 66, 67, 139. *See also*
Self-hatred
Interracial attitudes, 15, 16, 55, 56,
59, 60, 61, 64, 65, 66, 67, 68,
69-70, 71, 72, 75, 76, 78-79, 80,
81, 92, 98, 99, 103, 105, 128,
130, 131, 142; of black middle
class, 21, 27, 28, 43; of black
middle class toward whites, 28,
56, 64, 67, 70, 71, 78, 80, 103,
131
Interracial contact, 28-31, 53, 56,
57, 66, 72, 74-75, 76, 85, 91, 97,
98, 99, 103, 105, 130, 135-36,
137, 138, 139, 142